CW00971429

OSPREY COMBAT AIRCRAFT • 82

A-26 INVADER UNITS OF WORLD WAR 2

SERIES EDITOR: TONY HOLMES

OSPREY COMBAT AIRCRAFT • 82

A-26 INVADER UNITS OF WORLD WAR 2

JIM ROEDER

OSPREY
PUBLISHING

Front Cover
The 416th Bombardment Group (BG) was the first USAAF unit in the European Theatre of Operations to fully convert from the A-20 Havoc to the A-26 Invader during the autumn of 1944. By year-end the France-based group had swapped virtually all of its Havocs for Invaders, and it was heavily involved in providing tactical bomber support for the Allied push towards Germany. On 16 February 1945, the 416th BG bombed the Wehrmacht's ordnance depot at Unna, in Germany. One of the aircraft to participate in the mission was Lt Lou Prucha's A-26B-20-DL 41-39274 *Sugar Baby*. Prucha was amongst the original pilots assigned to the 668th Bomb Squadron (BS), and he had previously flown an A-20 that was also named *Sugar Baby*. According to the group's combat diary, 'Moderate to intense, accurate, flak followed the aeroplanes on their bomb run over the target, and on the turn-off. The most intense flak seemed to be coming from Dortmund and Hann'.

Three pilots subsequently received the Air Medal for bravery following this mission, including the 670th BS's Lt Bob Bower, who described the operation as follows;

'The flak was very, very intense and accurate. Everywhere I looked I saw flak. The sky just seemed to be filled with the lethal stuff. One curtain of it was so heavy that it seemed that someone had taken a black crayon and coloured out the blue sky. We encountered flak for about 15 minutes before we hit the target, as well as over the target itself and for about five minutes after we had left the target. Capt Bowman's gunner counted 250 bursts. My gunner called me and said "Wow! You should see the flak back here". For my part, I had all the flak in front of me that I ever wanted to see or hear about!'

The 416th BG's 671st BS lost one A-26 during this mission, the group's combat diary recording, 'Going in on the bomb run, the aeroplane flown by Flt Off H J Wilson, with Sgt E F Berkes as his gunner, was seen to nose up and then start downward, still under control. It went in the clouds at 6000 ft and has not been heard from since'.

DEDICATION

I would like to dedicate this book both to the memory of Jerry Scutts and to my younger brother David W Roeder Snr, who is losing his fight with cancer.

First published in Great Britain in 2010 by Osprey Publishing
Midland House, West Way, Botley, Oxford, OX2 0PH
44-02 23rd St, Suite 219, Long Island City, New York, 11101

E-mail; info@ospreypublishing.com

ISBN; 978 1 84603 431 2
E-book ISBN: 978 1 84908 130 6

Edited by Tony Holmes and Bruce Hales-Dutton
Page design by Tony Truscott
Cover Artwork by Mark Postlethwaite
Aircraft Profiles by Janusz Swiatlon
Index by Alan Thatcher
Originated by PDQ Digital Media Solutions, Suffolk, UK
Printed in China through Bookbuilders

10 11 12 13 14   10 9 8 7 6 5 4 3 2 1

Osprey Publishing is supporting the Woodland Trust, the UK's leading woodland conservation charity by funding the dedication of trees.

www.ospreypublishing.com

Lt Prucha's A-26B-20 41-139274 survived the war and was converted into a TB-26B dual-control pilot trainer. After more than a decade of USAAF/USAF service, it was one of a handful of Invaders supplied to the Cuban air force in 1956 (*Cover artwork by Mark Postlethwaite*)

CONTENTS

PREPARING THE INVADER

Built by Douglas, the A-26 Invader was a twin-engined, single pilot attack bomber that boasted a slight family resemblance to its predecessor, the A-20 Havoc, although it was considerably faster (with a maximum speed of 373 mph, versus 317 mph for the A-20). First flown on 10 July 1942, the A-26 was pronounced ready to enter service by the test pilot at the controls for this inaugural flight, Ben Howard. Yet, despite his enthusiasm, two years would pass before the Invader finally made its combat debut in July 1944 with the A-20-equipped 13th Bombardment Squadron (BS), 3rd Bomb Group (BG) in New Guinea.

Prior to engaging the enemy, the A-26 had been issued in growing numbers to units in the USA as air- and groundcrews gained experience on the new aircraft before commencing combat evaluation in the Pacific and European theatres. Pilots reported that the Invader was a stable,

Prototype XA-26 41-19504 is seen here at Mines Field, Los Angeles, on 29 April 1943. Its distinctive propeller spinners were not adopted when the aircraft entered production due to engine cooling problems that arose when they were fitted

Nacelles removed, an early-build A-26B receives routine maintenance in the open somewhere in the ETO in early 1945. The Pratt & Whitney R-2800-27 radial engines were readily accessible once their close-fitting nacelles had been unfastened and carefully taken off

reliable and pleasant aircraft to fly, although its long, broad nose and close engine placement drew criticism from Havoc pilots in the 13th BS, as they felt that both restricted their vision when flying at lower levels. Nevertheless, the A-26 possessed excellent single-engine flight characteristics, even if one of its Pratt & Whitney R-2800 Double Wasp radials failed on take-off. Once in action, it was found that the Invader could withstand considerable combat damage.

Another important attribute was that the A-26 aircrew requirement was one-third or even half that of any other medium or light bomber then in service with the USAAF. Just a pilot and rear gunner initially crewed the solid nose A-26B, and a bombardier/navigator was added with the advent of the A-26C with its Plexiglas nose section. The A-20 required a minimum of three aircrew, with a fourth added for the A-20J/K variants. As previously mentioned, the A-26B featured a solid nose housing six (increased to eight in later production A-26Bs) Browning 0.50-in machine guns. The A-26C had a Plexiglas nose section for a bombardier, with two 0.50-in guns mounted to starboard. The C-model was identical to the A-26B in all other respects, however.

Invaders were manufactured at two of Douglas' plants, with its Long Beach, California, facility building A-26Bs and five Plexiglas-nosed A-26Cs at the very start of the latter model's production run – these were the only only C-models built at Long Beach, with the remainder being assembled at the Tulsa, Oklahoma, plant which produced both B- and C-models concurrently. Fuselages for both variants were assembled on the same lines at Tulsa, but manufacturing delays in the early stages of Invader production resulted in a slow delivery rate to the USAAF. The reasons for these delays were numerous, and included (but were not limited to) the incorporation of new equipment, together with design and tooling difficulties.

Another hindrance was the large number of changes issued daily by the USAAF, which initially planned to replace all of its medium bomber aircraft with the Invader from late 1942. However, indecision as to the exact role the aircraft would fulfil resulted in myriad design changes and serious delays to its production schedule. Incorporating these changes in the production line

The Invader was built from the outset to be flown by a solitary pilot, unlike previous American medium and light bombers. This young second lieutenant was photographed in the cockpit of an A-26B during his conversion onto the aircraft with a stateside training unit. A jump seat was also usually provided for either the navigator or flight engineer. Note the gunsight fitted to the instrument panel

Fitted with an early flat top canopy, this A-26C was assigned to the 416th BG in the winter of 1944-45. The bombardier's feet can just be seen dangling through the open crew access hatch in the nose of the aircraft

without pause, along with other issues, caused the slow production rate. This initially resulted in more A-26Bs reaching the frontline. To ease the shortage of C-models in the USAAF, and to provide Invaders capable of carrying a bombardier, the Tulsa plant produced A-26C nose sections as field kits for units to install on existing A-26Bs. As many examples of the latter were fitted with a C-model nose, the serial number is the only certain way to determine if an A-26 was indeed built as a C-model, or was a B with a C nose added as a field modification.

While the Invader had many outstanding qualities, it also had its share of shortcomings. As previously mentioned, chief among them was restricted visibility due to the heavy canopy framing and the large size, and positioning, of the engine cowlings. Another was the fact that the primary means of cockpit entry and exit was through a hatch on the right side of the canopy. This hatch was hinged at the front and swung upwards and forwards, but there was a console containing instruments and switches in the centre of the cockpit so that while entry and exit was normally fairly easy, it could be difficult and extraordinarily time-consuming in an emergency.

Prior to the commencement of the Invader's combat evaluation in the Pacific, the issue of limited visibility had been recognised by Douglas to the point where it had introduced an interim fix on the Tulsa and Long Beach production lines in June 1944. This took the

Another early flat top Invader – this time an A-26B – provides the backdrop for personnel (both air- and groundcrew) from the 416th BG

Fitted with underwing gun pods, this A-26B suffered a nose gear failure whilst taxiing at Laon/Athies in early 1945. Both propellers have been badly damaged and the engines wrenched. The aircraft is also equipped with a large, heavily-framed hatch on the right-hand side of the canopy, which provided cockpit access. This early style hatch severely restricted pilot visibility

form of a single, unobstructed, curved section of Plexiglas in place of the framed panels above and to the left of the pilot. Referred to as the 'revised flat top canopy', this modification helped to increase the pilot's visibility forward but did not resolve the major issue of restricted vision over the engine cowlings. Apart from this simple alteration, the revised canopy was identical to the original 'flat top' fitted to the first production examples, and it was incorporated into the Long

In an effort to improve cockpit visibility, a revised canopy style was quickly introduced by Douglas. As this damaged machine from the 416th BG clearly shows, two framed panels on the left hand side of the canopy were replaced by a single large frameless panel

Beach line from the A-26B-20DL and A-26B-15DT models, as well as the A-26C-15DT at Tulsa.

Ultimately, a completely redesigned canopy was required to improve visibility. In August 1944 Douglas fitted an A-26 with a handmade canopy, its two moulded and frameless hatches boasting a distinct upward bulge over the cockpit. The hatches were hinged at their bottom edges and opened outwards like a clamshell. Naturally, the 'revised bubble canopy' came to be known as the 'clamshell canopy'. When viewed from the side, the canopy angled upwards from the fuselage then dropped slightly downwards to meet the windscreen. The higher canopy also allowed the pilot's seat mounting to be raised, which in turn provided greater visibility over the engine nacelles. It also made exiting the aircraft in an emergency both faster and safer.

The introduction of a new component such as this into an active production line could easily result in serious disruption, so it was not until December 1944 that new aircraft fitted with the clamshell canopy started to leave the Douglas plants. Previous publications on the A-26 have stated that the new clamshell canopy was retrofitted to earlier Invaders fitted with the original flat style canopy. However, the author has conducted extensive research in company literature and maintenance manuals, and pored over hundreds of production line photographs, and none have revealed evidence to support this belief. Interviews with air- and groundcrews have failed to confirm this either.

The reason for this apparent error may be, quite simply, a case of mistaken identity due to a confusion of terms. That is, confusing the revised flat top canopy with the new revised bubble canopy. The revised flat top panel could easily be installed on aircraft completed before the introduction of the revised bubble canopy, groundcrew simply removing the screws that held the original framed canopy in place and then replacing it with the flat top panel. This switch could be accomplished without the A-26 having to be taken out of service. The clamshell canopy could not be installed on aircraft completed with the flat top canopy, however, as the redesigned component was higher at the front than at the rear and the angle of the front windscreen was altered. To even attempt to replace the flat top canopy with the revised bubble one would have required time-consuming and extensive metal and Plexiglas work far in excess of any potential benefit. There are examples of the A-26 Invader

Much wind tunnel-testing was undertaken by Douglas to ensure that the nacelle design created the least amount of drag possible whilst still providing sufficient airflow for engine cooling

built with the original flat top canopy still in existence today, never having had their canopy assemblies replaced.

Although the new clamshell canopy was vastly superior to its flat top predecessor, it had a flaw nevertheless. On flat canopy A-26s, the upper turret could be locked forward and fired by the pilot, but the increased height of the new clamshell transparency eliminated that option.

A further misconception is that the Invader could switch from being a level bomber to a ground strafer simply by replacing the Plexiglas nose with the six- or eight-gun solid nose. No evidence to support that belief has been found to date. Indeed, to attempt such a task in the field would have been far too time-consuming for the groundcrew involved. With the underwing 0.50-in gun pods (two weapons per pod) or wing-mounted guns (three within each wing), even the glazed-nosed A-26C could be used for strafing missions – life for the bombardier during such strafing attacks would probably have been quite interesting!

The A-26 was armed with two turrets, each mounting two 0.50-in machine guns that were controlled remotely by the gunner housed in a compartment just aft of the bomb-bay. These turrets were similar to those used in the B-29. Rotation of the turrets, as well as the elevation, depression and firing of the guns, was accomplished through the use of hand controls. Sighting was via a periscope that projected both above and below the gunner's compartment. The gunner's seat was attached to the periscope and it rotated via a circular track in the floor.

Aside from the A-26B's solid nose containing six 0.50-in machine guns, additional forward firepower was initially provided by single underwing pods housing a further pair of 0.50-in machine guns. These added considerable drag to the aircraft, however, reducing its top speed by 25 mph. This problem was rectified when Douglas began producing aircraft with three 0.50-in guns mounted in the leading edge of each wing, the barrel of the centre weapon projecting out further than the other two. This arrangement increased the Invader's firepower without adversely affecting its airspeed.

Late production A-26B/Cs featured wing hard points for the mounting of eight five-inch high-velocity aerial rockets under each wing, as well as a rack for a bomb or external fuel tank. The fixed armament in the nose of the A-26B was also subsequently increased to eight 0.50-in machine guns, arranged in two vertical rows of four guns. This fit was introduced on the production line with the A-26B-55DL, and the new eight-gun

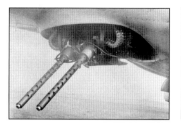

The remotely operated ventral gun turret, seen here with its domed cover removed to allow the weapons to be serviced

The dorsal turret of this aircraft has also had its inner workings exposed for the benefit of the camera. The twin 0.50-in Browning machine guns have been locked in the forward position in this early-build A-26B

A 416th BG A-26B is rearmed at Laon/Athies in early 1945

The Mk 33 bomb sighting unit as fitted in the Invader. A. denotes the precision latch, B. the action switch (bomb release trigger) and C. the elevation latch

Fresh off the Long Beach production line, A-26B-45-DL 44-34216 performs a check flight prior to being handed over to the USAAF in early 1945

nose was also made available as a field modification kit. The lower turret was deleted from the A-26C-55DT and A-26B-50DL onward, an extra fuel tank being installed in the fuselage in its place. Ironically, the added external rocket and bomb capability would prove to be of little benefit to the A-26 because operations in rough field conditions caused a weakening of the wing structure when laden down with ordnance.

The Invader was also plagued with nose gear failures. This issue is well known, and there are photographs published in this book that show the end result of such failures. The cause has at least two known origins, both of which were remedied. The first was traced to undue stress being placed on the nose wheel and strut by attempts to turn the aircraft while it was not moving forwards. This is like starting a car, then turning the steering wheel to make a turn before putting it into gear and moving forwards, thereby placing a strain on the steering mechanism. The A-26's nose wheel strut could not withstand the stresses involved. The remedy was to instruct pilots – and to include instructions on a placard on the instrument panel as well as in the pilot's manual – to begin taxiing forwards before attempting to turn the aircraft.

The other cause was the weather, combined with conditions at European advanced landing fields during the autumn and winter of 1944-45. Mud, snow and debris clogged the folding actions and hinges of the nose and main landing gears, resulting in sudden failure. Crashes on take-off and landing caused by gear failure were quite common, and it was not unusual for several accidents to befall a unit due to bad weather in a single day. While measures were taken to counter these failures, total elimination could not be achieved.

COMBAT EVALUATION

In early 1944 the 3rd BG's 13th BS was selected to evaluate the Invader in combat in the Pacific. Based at Hollandia, New Guinea, the group had flown its A-20s in low-level attacks on Japanese land and sea forces, and it completed its scheduled A-26 evaluation in July 1944. Issued with four Invaders, pilots from the 13th criticised the aircraft's flat, heavily framed canopy. They also found that the size and positioning of the engine nacelles not only restricted visibility, but also made low-level formation flying and manoeuvring dangerous. In combat, these dangers increased almost exponentially, requiring crews to remain constantly aware of each others' location.

Another less sinister criticism was that the aircraft's cruising speed was considerably greater than that of the A-20, which meant that both types could not be used in the same combat formation. Both Douglas and the USAAF were aware of these issues, and measures were already in hand to correct them. In fact, apart from the canopy problems, almost all the deficiencies listed by the 3rd BG had been identified by Douglas before the start of the combat evaluation.

The aircraft would not be used in further operations by the 3rd BG, or any other unit based in the Pacific, until the early summer of 1945. This was not due to any shortcomings in the aircraft, as has been speculated in other publications. Indeed, it had never been the USAAF's intention to immediately convert the 3rd BG, or any Pacific Theatre, unit to the A-26. Instead, it simply wanted to evaluate the aircraft's combat performance and correct any deficiencies that arose from these trials.

The Invader's delayed arrival in the Pacific has often been misconstrued as a complete rejection of the A-26 by the 3rd BG, which was not the case. The intended assignment of the aircraft to the Fifth Air Force was not received favourably by its commanding officer, Gen George Kenney, who stated emphatically that he did not want the A-26 as a replacement for any aircraft for any reason. This comment was not made because of any major shortcomings with the Invader, but was based on Kenney's firm belief that the A-20s and B-25s then equipping his groups were more than sufficient for their assigned purpose. His view was both logically and logistically sound. A greater number of different aircraft types designed for essentially the same purpose required a correspondingly extended inventory of spare parts. Kenney was not alone in his efforts to standardise on a specific type or types of aircraft within his command.

The USAAF eventually decided to send the A-26 into combat in the Pacific towards the end of the war. The first group selected to use it would be the 319th BG, not the 3rd BG, and the group would not reach Okinawa until early July 1945. The 3rd commenced its conversion in the

This A-26B-35-DL was assigned to a stateside training unit, but precisely which one remains something of a mystery. Such outfits were dotted all over the southern states, as well as on the west coast

Although this A-26B displays the markings of the 386th BG, it is actually one of the 18 Project Squadron aircraft attached to the unit in August 1944. This photograph was taken while the 416th BG was converting to the A-26. During the initial conversion training period, Project Squadron aircraft retained the 386th BG markings used during the evaluation missions

early summer of 1945, and the group would subsequently operate both the A-26 and A-20 in the offensive against Formosa in June-July.

ETO EVALUATIONS

Evaluation missions in the ETO were conducted in a different manner to those in the Pacific. Instead of deploying a handful of aircraft, the USAAF decided to use an entire squadron staffed by experienced crews that had been trained in the USA on the A-26 to form an independent unit. This Project Squadron was formed specifically to evaluate the Invader by flying a series of combat missions, after which it would be attached to other units in the ETO to assist them in their conversion to the aircraft.

The men selected to form the new unit came from Barksdale Field, Louisiana, which was home to the B-26 Marauder combat crew transition school. 18 crews (18 pilots, six bombardier/navigators and 18 gunners) were selected from the instructor crews to fly the A-26 combat evaluation missions in Europe. Under Special Orders No 205, Project 3AF JY 30 Class TM 0725, the 18 crews were formed into the A-26 Combat Evaluation Project Squadron. Maj Howard Burhanna was appointed Project Squadron leader, and he remained in this position until he was assigned to the 416th BG in October 1944. The crews reported to Hunter Field, Georgia, to pick up 18 brand new Invaders (12 B-models and six A-26Cs) before flying to Prestwick, Scotland, in early August 1944. From there the group headed south to Ninth Air Force Station 164 at Great Dunmow, Essex, base of the B-26 Marauder-equipped 386th BG.

There, the Project Squadron was attached – not assigned – to the 553rd BS for the sole purpose of evaluating the A-26 in combat. That the unit was attached and not assigned is an important distinction, as each term has a specific definition in the US armed forces. At times entire or partial units, even individuals, were attached to another unit for a specific purpose or reason. The host unit supplied the logistical needs such as ordnance, clerical, messing or maintenance of the unit or personnel attached, who in turn still retained their autonomy, in an arrangement that in civilian life might be considered a 'marriage of convenience'. After the specific reason or purpose of the attachment was satisfied, the attached unit or personnel either returned to their parent organisation or were attached or assigned to another unit. All 18 crews within the A-26 Combat Evaluation Project Squadron remained under the command of Maj Burhanna, and they were never led by anyone in the 386th BG.

The landing accident that has befallen this Project Squadron A-26 has revealed the D-Day bands applied to the underside of the fuselage forward of the ventral turret

Once at Great Dunmow, the Invaders were given a thorough inspection and adorned with the markings of the 386th BG. The application of the latter has caused some historians to assume that the aircraft were actually assigned to that group, thus making it the first to receive the A-26. Neither the aircraft nor the crews of the Project Squadron were assigned to the 386th BG, nor were they absorbed by it in any way.

As it happens, there was an enigma resulting from the application of the required markings and insignia, as invasion (or D-Day) stripes were painted on the lower aft fuselage of the A-26s. On 5 June 1944, all Allied aircraft (except B-17s and B-24s) had the invasion stripes applied to the rear fuselage, as well as to the upper and lower surfaces of both wings, to identify them as friendly to Allied forces. However, they were not displayed by new aircraft received in the ETO from the end of June. By July the stripes were being removed from the upper fuselage and upper wings, and by September the stripes only remained on the lower fuselages of most aircraft. Yet photographs show several A-26s of the 409th and 416th BGs displaying stripes on their lower fuselages well after October. The reason for this remains a mystery, although it may have been driven by the crews' desire for self-preservation. The A-26 was a new aircraft, not only to the inventory but also to the ETO, so as Allied (as well as German) forces were accustomed to seeing these stripes, they may have been applied to avoid attracting 'friendly fire'.

During the author's research into the A-26's ETO combat evaluation, conflicting information has come to light. The following account conflicts with other documentation relating both to the evaluation itself and to the type's subsequent assignment to combat units in-theatre. Both accounts are related in their entirety because of the inaccurate impression that could result from reading either without further research into the matter. In 1944, Lt Col Ted Hankey was assigned to the 386th BG at Great Dunmow, and his recollections were included in *The Crusaders*, a unit history published by the 386th BG Association. Hankey recalled;

'I was scheduled to go home in August 1944. Some time around the first of the month Maj Gen Samuel E Anderson, CO of the Ninth Bombardment Division, called me in and told me that there was a new aeroplane on the way, the A-26, and that it would be assigned to the 386th BG. He asked me to take charge of the unit, which had been trained at Barksdale, and lead them on the first five missions, and then I could go home. The squadron was preceded by a colonel, who had trained the unit. He was convinced that the A-26 would win the war single-handedly. He told us how it could bomb at medium altitude and strafe. None of us with combat experience in the Marauder believed it, and some very heated arguments ensued, almost ending in a fist fight when the colonel squared off against Capt Al Hill, one of our lead bombardiers.

A Project Squadron A-26B lands at Great Dunmow during the Invader's combat evaluation in the autumn of 1944

'The day arrived when we got a call that the squadron had left Prestwick for Great Dunmow. I gave them a few hours and headed over to the tower with their commander to welcome them to the 386th. It was a typical English day, with scud blowing around the field at 1500 ft and two layers of overcast above that. It had been raining and the runway was slippery and the Essex mud alongside even worse.

'From the tower we began to pick up their chatter, the essence being, "Where the hell are we and where is the field?" I got on the radio on the pre-set frequency and tried to make contact. I never got through to anyone in spite of repeating over and over that they were over our field. Then a couple of them came into our view and entered the traffic pattern. The first one landed long, used too much brake and slid sideways off the end of the runway, across the perimeter track and into the mud. From then on it was a complete fiasco. I can't remember the order in which it happened but one ended up in the mud on the right side of the runway about halfway down and perpendicular to it with his nose just over the edge. One landing was so bad that the aeroplane hit the A-26 that was in the mud to the right of the runway with his left wing. He had to have been at least 70 ft out in the mud to have achieved this.

'In the tower we were telling them to go around. We had the landing hut at the end of the runway firing so many flares it looked like the 4th of July! All of this was ignored and in they came. Some hit the bogged aeroplane at the end of the runway, and in all six were damaged, three of which had the glass noses that meant they could be used as lead ships. Needless to say the squadron commander was unimpressed. As the squadron was totally my responsibility per Gen Anderson, I called the A-26 pilots together and grounded the lot. Those that had landed safely I used to check out the 553rd, which was the first squadron to get A-26s. Then they were given a quick check and used for co-pilots on the B-26s.

'We held five briefings for the A-26s, but due to the weather did not get any of them off. We finally got one off to Brest on 6 September against some strong points as I recall. I reported to Gen Anderson what I had done with the squadron, and that the aeroplane was practically no different to the B-26 in respect to the way that we would use them. He told me to forget the other four missions and go home.'

While conducting research into the introduction and first use of the A-26 in the ETO, the author received information that contradicted the preceding account. In fairness, both are related. Hankey implies that the A-26 pilots and their commander were both insubordinate and incompetent, and that he grounded all 18. By stating 'as the squadron was totally my responsibility per Gen Anderson', he implies that he was CO of the Project Squadron, which he was not. Hankey also claims that he used the A-26 pilots who landed safely to check out the 553rd BS on the Invader, and that squadron subsequently became the first to receive the A-26. He states that he then reassigned the 12 pilots to the 553rd as B-26 co-pilots. No further mention is made of the six whom he said did not land safely.

Shortly after the author received the preceding account, contact was made with the last surviving member of the Project Squadron. Lt Francis 'Sandy' Brewster was an instructor pilot at Barksdale Field when he was assigned to the Project Squadron to evaluate the aircraft in combat in the ETO. Brewster stated that during his service as a USAAF officer and pilot he was never assigned as a B-26 co-pilot by Col Hankey, grounded or court-martialled. Furthermore, grounding one pilot, let alone 18, would have required administrative action and not merely a unilateral and verbal order.

The runways at Great Dunmow were indeed wet when the Project Squadron arrived from Prestwick, resulting in several accidents during landing. These accidents were due to conditions beyond the control of the arriving pilots, and not due to their deliberately ignoring instructions from control tower personnel. Weather-induced poor runway conditions were not exclusive to bases in England. The advanced landing grounds in Europe were also routinely compromised by inclement weather. Small rocks and other debris, as well as ice and standing water, were often present on runways and taxiways.

Individual pilots could be, and were, qualified to fly the A-26 after a short period of tuition by instructor pilots. However, completely retraining an entire squadron in less than two weeks was not possible, as was learned later during the conversion of the 416th BG to the Invader. Conversion training involved not only pilots but

Armourers carefully winch a 500-lb (GP) bomb into the bomb-bay of a Project Squadron Invader at Great Dunmow

The Project Squadron suffered a high attrition rate due to undercarriage failures whilst in the ETO. An aircraft such as this could be repaired, however

The 386th BG did not undertake its conversion from the Marauder to the Invader until early 1945. Here, a mixed formation of A-26Bs and Cs heads for a target in western Germany

gunners, navigators, mechanics and other support personnel required to work on the new aircraft. A mobile training unit accompanied instructor aircrews and conducted the training of the other personnel.

The periscope gunsight remote control system for the gun turrets, as well as the turrets themselves, were new to B-26 units. The groundcrews also required instruction in the maintenance of the turrets, gunsights and other new equipment. Converting an entire group to a brand new aircraft proved to be time consuming as no other light or medium bomber in service had any, let alone all, of these new features. Only one other aircraft in the entire USAAF inventory had similar or identical systems and that was the B-29, which was classified as a very heavy bomber and involved a training programme even more complex than that of the A-26. Hankey's account may have resulted from a memory lapse, for no documentation has so far been found to support it, while documentation to contradict it has surfaced.

ETO COMBAT EVALUATION MISSIONS

On 6 September 1944 the first A-26 ETO combat mission was flown by the Project Squadron crews against German strong points at Brest. The remainder of the evaluation missions were undertaken over the next two weeks. On the 10th the Project Squadron targeted a bridge at Nancy and the third and fourth missions were flown the following day, the first of these being against German gun positions at Metz. The third mission (the day's second) was an attack on the Luftwaffe airfield at Leeuwarden, in Holland. The fifth mission, on 12 September, saw the aircraft strike fortifications at Sheld, while the sixth, on the 14th, was a return attack on enemy strong points in Brest. Two days later the A-26s bombed the Berg op Zoom dyke in Holland. The eighth, and final, evaluation mission was against marshalling yards at Duren.

After the completion of the evaluation missions, the Project Squadron detached from the 386th BG and left Great Dunmow for Station 170 Wethersfield soon afterwards. Once at the latter base, the unit commenced the conversion of the 416th BG from the A-20 to the A-26. During the last week of September, the 386th BG moved from Great Dunmow to Advanced Landing Ground A569 at Laon, in

Below and bottom
The nose gear of this A-26B collapsed on landing after a training mission at Wethersfield on 18 October 1944. This is one of at least three landing gear failures known to have occurred on the same day and at the same location

Below and bottom
The nose gear of this A-26B collapsed on landing after a training mission at Wethersfield on 18 October 1944. This is one of at least three landing gear failures known to have occurred on the same day and at the same location

17

France. From there the group would continue to fly combat missions with its B-26 Marauders until early 1945, when it converted to the A-26.

During preparations for Operation *Overlord,* the need for a UK-based tactical air force to provide support for the invasion forces, and later the Allied armies as they advanced across Europe, was recognised. In August 1943 the Ninth Air Force was transferred from the Mediterranean theatre to England to fill this role. Of its 11 bomb groups, three were classified as light bomb groups and flew the A-20 Havoc, while the remaining eight, equipped with B-26 Marauders, were designated as medium bomb groups. It was these combat groups that were selected to be the first in the USAAF to convert to the A-26 Invader.

While the eight evaluation missions flown by the Project Squadron in the first half of September 1944 were successful, the aircraft was not employed in the low-level bombing/strafing or medium altitude bombing roles for which it had been developed. As a result, many crews considered the Invader to offer little improvement over their beloved B-26 when used as a medium bomber. Indeed, Ninth Air Force commander Gen Hoyt Vandenburg noted that the A-26 was better suited to the role being filled by the A-20. It was therefore decided to re-equip the three Ninth Air Force Havoc units ahead of the Marauder groups.

The war in Europe ended before all the USAAF's medium bomb groups could be re-equipped, and those that were assigned to the Occupation of Germany Forces post VE Day swapped their Marauders for Invaders during the summer of 1945.

One other Ninth Air Force unit contributed to the medium bomb groups' effectiveness with the A-20, B-26 and A-26. This was the 1st Pathfinder (PFF) Squadron, which provided the groups with PFF-equipped Marauders. These aircraft led the medium bombers when a target was expected to be obscured by bad weather. The PFF Marauders would rendezvous with the bombers at a specific time and location, then lead them to the target. The bombardier in the PFF aircraft would transmit a signal at the moment of bomb release to the following bombers, which would then drop their own ordnance. After bomb release it would depart and return to its own base. As weather prevented visual sighting of the target, observation of the results was not usually possible.

A-26B-15-DL was assigned to the 386th BG's 553rd BS from early 1945. The aircraft survived the war and later appeared on the US civil register as N5245V

INTO ACTION

As previously noted, after the conclusion of the evaluation missions the Project Squadron moved to Wethersfield, home of the 416th BG. The latter had been the Ninth Air Force's first A-20-equipped group, and it duly became the first to convert to the A-26 – two distinctions its personnel were proud of.

The Project Squadron's arrival coincided with the 416th's move to A55 Melun, in France, in mid September 1944. Conversion to the new aircraft and movement of the unit would be accomplished concurrently. As priorities were elsewhere at the time, the A-26s initially retained the markings of the 386th BG, which they wore during evaluation missions. It is uncertain exactly where and when they were changed, but the aircraft displayed 416th BG markings by the time they flew their first mission from Melun. The invasion stripes on the lower fuselage were retained, and several A-26s received in October also displayed the stripes.

Combat is often described as being a fluid environment, which it most certainly is. While conditions can and do change suddenly, there are some things that remain fairly constant, however. The weather in England and Europe during the Invader's time in the ETO often changed from bad to worse, hindering flight operations, let alone the completion of a mission.

Reviews of mission information recorded in the official histories and reports from the units involved were remarkable for describing what was not encountered as much as what was. Flak was not always present, and when it was the accuracy and amount varied considerably. Encounters with German fighters were rarely mentioned, and at least one A-26 pilot stated the he never saw an enemy aircraft in any of his 65 missions.

There exists a plausible explanation for this. By the autumn of 1944 the Luftwaffe was being progressively crippled by insufficient fuel supplies and a paucity of pilots. With logistical problems increasing exponentially each day, it was forced to prioritise in an attempt to effectively utilise its quickly dwindling resources and infrastructure. The stopping, or at the very least hindrance, of daily bombing raids by the B-17s and B-24s of the Eighth and Fifteenth Air Forces became a major issue for the shrinking Luftwaffe. This in turn meant that available fighters were ordered to engage the 'heavies' and leave the medium bombers alone, as the shooting down of a B-17 or B-24 was deemed more important than the destruction of several A-26s, A-20s or B-26s. As a result, the medium bomb groups did not encounter fighters on every mission.

That is not to say, however, that these missions were 'milk runs' because they were unopposed by fighters. The Wehrmacht still had plenty of anti-aircraft guns (*Flugzeug-Abwehr-Kannonen* or flak guns) and shells for them to oppose Allied bombers, no matter what their size. What the Germans lacked was sufficient fuel for their aircraft and vehicles.

The 416th BG would see more combat in the A-26 than any other unit in the USAAF in World War 2, so it is only fitting that its exploits should provide the bulk of this volume's narrative.

In late September 1944 the Project Squadron arrived at Wethersfield to begin the 416th BG's transition to the A-26. The group had been flying combat missions with the A-20 from Wethersfield since 3 March 1944 as the Ninth Air Force's first light bomb group. The Havoc was being used by three of the Ninth's 11 bomb groups by the autumn of that year, and all of them operated the same variants of the A-20, namely the G-, H-, J- and K-models. The G- and H-models were identical, each having a solid nose section mounting four 0.50-in machine guns and a Martin turret with two 0.50-in weapons on the upper rear fuselage. The major difference between the two models was the type of engine used, with the G-model featuring two Wright R-2600-23 Double Cyclone rated at 1600 hp each, and the A-20H the R-2600-29 of 1700 hp.

The A-20J/K had the solid nose replaced by a frameless glazed nose section that contained a Norden bombsight and a bombardier. The aircraft retained the Martin upper turret. As with the G- and H-models, the major difference between the A-20J and K centred on their engines.

Shortly after the Project Squadron arrived at Wethersfield, the 416th began moving to France. The Allies had broken through the German defensive lines in the late summer of 1944 and had started moving towards the Fatherland itself. At the same time the Ninth Air Force began deploying its fighter and bomber groups to bases in France to provide support for the ground forces. The transition training for the 416th was conducted concurrently with the group's move to Melun.

On 17 September the 416th BG crews awaiting A-26 training began flying combat missions from Melun with the A-20. In October a new procedure for transition training was instituted that saw each of the four squadrons take one flight of four aircraft, and their crews, off operational duties for conversion training to the A-26. The associated groundcrews were also trained in maintaining the aircraft. By the second week of October it was realised that this method was far too time-consuming to be practical, so one entire squadron was instead removed from operations to convert to the A-26 en masse. On the 17th, the 670th BS became the group's first squadron to complete its conversion to the A-26.

The next squadron selected for conversion was the 671st. The unit's crews began conversion in a marathon schedule that started just before dawn and lasted until after dark each day. The combination of bad weather and an intense training schedule resulted in several incidents, although one at least had its lighter side. A newly trained A-26 pilot took off on a training flight over the Melun area but the weather suddenly closed in, shutting the airfield to operations. The pilot was forced to fly in a westerly direction in an attempt to find an alternative landing ground. After some time he found one that was in clear weather, so he entered the recovery pattern and landed. On reporting to field operations, he discovered that he was in England, not France! After a short time, pilot, crew and aircraft returned to Melun, no longer listed as missing in action.

Bad weather and enemy action were not the only causes of aircraft losses, however, for on 19 October an A-26 was damaged when its nose wheel failed on landing. Such failures plagued Invader units through to war's end, as noted in chapter one.

While retraining a whole squadron at the same time appeared to be the quickest way to transition the 416th BG onto the A-26, it was soon

A 416th BG pilot scrutinises paperwork presented to him by his crew chief detailing rectification work that has been carried out on his aircraft since the last mission. If the pilot was happy that all was in order, he would sign the documentation and duly take the aircraft aloft on its next mission

A groundcrewman refuels a 416th BG A-26 at Melun. It is not clear why there is only one gun in each underwing pod, although such an arrangement was seen in photographs of several 416th BG Invaders

discovered to be impractical. On 3 November, therefore, the entire group was taken off operations to begin conversion to the Invader. The following day most of the 416th's remaining A-20s were flown to England and 40 A-26Bs received in return. Once again, bad weather hampered operations, delaying their return until the 6th.

Lt Bart Singletary of the 671st was one of the pilots who collected a new A-26B. An experienced 416th A-20 pilot, he was also a flight leader. After a briefing from an instructor pilot, and with his crew chief advising on flap settings, approach and landing speeds and other vital information, he flew back to Melun. The 416th stood down for the next three days while the new aircraft underwent thorough acceptance inspections.

With a shortage of A-26Cs in the ETO at this time, the group retained a number of glazed-nosed A-20J/Ks for use as lead aircraft on level bombing missions. One Havoc, sometimes with a second A-20 as deputy lead, would head up each flight of A-26Bs. The A-20 bombardier releasing his bombs was the signal for the Invaders to do the same. P-38 groups of the Eighth and Ninth Air Forces used a similar approach. A Lightning modified with a glazed nose to house a bombardier would lead a squadron of P-38s on level bombing missions, and when the lead bombardier dropped his bombs, the following pilots released theirs too.

Winter arrived at the end of October, and with it came bad weather and shortened days. During winter months the average amount of daylight was 7 hrs 45 min, which contrasted with the average amount of daylight (16 hrs 25 min) during the summer. Limited light levels combined with bad weather to adversely affect the results of the combat missions.

Using A-20J/Ks as flight leaders, the 416th BG flew its first A-26 mission on 17 November when it was sent to bomb Haguenau, on the French-German border. Light rain was already falling at Melun when the aircraft took off, and by the time they reached the target area conditions had deteriorated, forcing the group to descend to a lower altitude in search of clear weather. The group had descended to 8000 ft before finding weather over the target clear enough to bomb accurately. The flak was weak and inaccurate and no enemy fighters were encountered. The 416th was one of six bomb groups flying missions that day, and they were all affected by poor weather. Indeed, of the six, only the 416th was able to see and bomb the target. The results were rated as satisfactory. Because of the bad weather, the other groups were unable to bomb their alternate targets either and they returned to their bases.

On 18 November the 416th flew its second A-26 mission. The official histories for three of the group's squadrons list the day's target as being the railway bridge at Breisach, in Germany, although for unknown reasons the official history of the 670th BS says it was the town of Durwiss. In any case, the bridge remained intact but the approaches to it were heavily damaged, rendering both the line and bridge unserviceable. The 669th BS history states that 'Capt Peck and Lt Madefort (bombardier/navigator) had trouble with the bombsight releasing the bombs on three attempts over the target. They finally decided to make a run on the town of Gebweiler. The bombs were released this time, with excellent results'.

On the 19th the 416th BG flew two more missions. The first of these saw 41 A-26s and eight A-20s sent to bomb German strong points at Merzig. Bad weather forced crews to attack from 6000 ft, with results rated as excellent. Flak was reported as 'ranging from light to heavy', but in the main it was 'weak and inaccurate', and no enemy fighters were encountered. The afternoon mission was supposed to attack the ordnance depot at Landau, but bad weather prevented identification of the target and the aircraft returned to Melun with their bomb loads still intact.

On 29 November the 416th targeted the defended village of Mariaweiler, although once again it was spared due to bad weather. Despite the group being prevented from bombing, the anti-aircraft batteries defending the target were not hindered by the weather, and the flak was said to have been both heavy and accurate. Indeed, the A-26B flown by Lt McBride of the 670th BS was hit and it caught fire, forcing both he and his gunner, SSgt Eustler, to bail out over friendly territory. Both men landed safely near Florennes-Juzaine. Shortly after their escape the aircraft exploded and crashed near Ciney, having become the first A-26 lost to enemy action during World War 2. It would not be the last.

The group bombed the fortified border town of Saarlautern on 2 December, and the results it achieved were rated as superior after hits were observed on roads and factory buildings. Crews reported the flak to be moderate but accurate. The mission flown three days later was led by a PFF-equipped B-26 Marauder, and the following A-26s dropped their bombs on its signal on the defended village of Kall, with the results being rated as good – no flak was reported. 6 December's mission was also PFF-led, and this time the defended village of Erkelenz came under attack – flak was reported as meagre. Although the bombing results were unobserved by the crews, photo-reconnaissance the next day showed them to have been superior. Half of the buildings in the north of the town had been damaged or destroyed and ten railway lines severed.

Armourers use a bomb trolley to manoeuvre a 500 'pounder' towards A-26B-15-DT 43-22378 at Melun in the autumn of 1944

Another 416th BG A-26B is prepared for a mission in France. This particular aircraft has two guns in each of its underwing pods

Sinzig railway bridge was the target on 8 December, but cloud cover prevented observation of the results. Post-mission photo-reconnaissance showed that the bombs had fallen beyond the bridge, however. During their return to base, the aircraft encountered flak that was reported as light but moderately accurate. The A-26 flown by Lt Grunig was hit and an engine knocked out, but thanks to the aircraft's excellent single-engine performance the pilot made it back to Melun. Two PFF-led missions followed the next day, with the morning raid targeting Saarwellin – bombing results were unobserved. The afternoon target was the defended village of Dilsburg, but PFF equipment in the lead B-26 malfunctioned and heavy cloud cover prevented visual bombing from taking place.

The defended village of Scheiden was the target of a PFF-led mission on 12 December, but again the specialist equipment failed. Following A-26 crews had been briefed to bomb only on a signal from the PFF aircraft, so no ordnance was expended and all the aircraft returned to base. The group bombed the defended village of Gemund from 12,500 ft using PFF methods on the 13th, although this was not its primary target – the latter had been obscured by bad weather, preventing observation of the results on Gemund. Two days later the defended village of Heimbach was attacked during a PFF mission. All aircraft bombed but solid cloud cover over the target precluded visual observation of the results.

On 16 December the Wehrmacht began its last desperate counter-offensive in the west. Centred on the Ardennes forest, it became known as the Battle of the Bulge. The Germans attempted to exploit a weakness in the Allied lines and hoped to capture the port of Antwerp. If this had been accomplished Allied forces would have been split in two and severely weakened. The weather which had so hampered the activities of Allied aircraft was exploited by the Germans. Shortly after the offensive began, Allied units were notified that English-speaking German soldiers wearing US uniforms and impersonating American soldiers of all ranks were infiltrating Allied lines and units. Their mission included the disruption of communications and supplies. Many of these soldiers were captured and executed as spies under the terms of the Geneva Convention. All personnel regardless of rank or job were required to wear full field gear and carry arms at all times until further notice.

At 0830 hrs on 23 December, with the battle at its height, the 416th BG commenced the first of two missions that it flew during the course of the day. Taking off at 0830 hrs, crews targeted a road bridge at Saarburg, ten miles south of Trier. The group attacked in a formation that consisted of eight flights, each of which was led by an A-20J/K. Flying at altitudes up to 12,000 ft, the first and second flights could not identify their aiming point as they neared the bridge.

Trailing smoke from a flak hit in its right engine, a 416th BG A-26B leaves the target area during the Battle of the Bulge in late December 1944

Electing to make a second run, the two flights circled around, by which time the third, fourth and fifth flights had identified the bridge and bombed it successfully.

During the bomb run, the A-20 leading the fifth flight was hit in the left engine by flak. With fire and smoke pouring from the engine, the pilot made a Herculean effort to control his aircraft and maintain his approach to the target. His bombs missed the bridge and struck nearby buildings, however. Realising that his A-20 was too badly damaged to make it back to Melun, the pilot crash-landed near Rheims. Bombs dropped by the sixth flight hit the bridge, with results rated as superior. The seventh and eighth flights' efforts were also judged to be excellent, destroying the bridge. By this time the first and second flights had commenced their second attack, bombing closely behind the seventh and eighth flights. The group returned to their base at Melun after an elapsed mission time of three hours. The only loss of the day for the 416th BG was the A-20 that crash-landed at Rheims.

At 1430 hrs the 416th sent 37 aircraft to bomb the communications centre at Waxweiler. Over the target area the group encountered light and inaccurate flak, but only one flight was able to bomb the primary target. The official history of the 668th BS reports that the 'other flights developed difficulties and bombed casual targets'. Exactly what these difficulties were is not mentioned, although the history goes on to state that 'Our group was very lucky on this morning's mission. Several other groups on reaching their target were beset by fighters and havoc ensued. Fate smiled on us as not a single enemy aeroplane was seen. Other groups had a hellish time'. The mission lasted 3 hrs 15 min, with all aircraft returning. Although five had been hit by flak, none were badly damaged.

On the afternoon of Christmas Eve the 416th sent 43 aircraft to attack the communications centre at Zulpich. This was the 175th combat mission flown by the group since its arrival in England in February 1944, and the official history of the 668th BS states that;

'This was a military objective of prime importance and would be prominent in halting the German drive. The orders were to get that target and get it dead centre. The formation was met with heavy flak but proceeded to make the bomb run. One A-26 was hit but continued on to drop its load. After releasing the bombs it crashed. One parachute was seen to land near the crashed aircraft. The rest of the formation returned to the base intact, although 11 aircraft had been flak damaged. The results were very gratifying.'

Sadly, not even Christmas Day was spared from the evils of war in 1944, with the A-26s of 416th BG flying two more missions. Early in the morning, 35 aircraft were sent to bomb the communications centre and motor transport repair centre at Bad Münstereifel. According to the 669th BS history, the flight was uneventful until the formation

Various airfield support equipment can be seen in this photograph of a 416th BG A-26B undergoing an engine change in the open

A formation of 670th BS/416th BG A-26s bombs through scattered cloud cover in late 1944. The formation is led by a PFF Marauder (out of shot), and the following Invaders have bombed on its signal

neared the target itself, where heavy and accurate flak was encountered. Moments before the release of its bombs, the A-20J flown by flight leader Capt Miracle was struck in the bomb-bay and the aircraft exploded in mid-air. Some crews reported observing a parachute being deployed but there were no survivors. Capt Miracle, who was flying his 69th mission, was one of several graduates of the US Military Academy, West Point, assigned to the 416th BG at that time. Lt Burg was Miracle's bombardier on this occasion. The official history of the 670th BS noted;

'Two missions on Christmas Day kept everyone busy. The first was an attack on the Munstereifel communications centre and the town itself. Only one flight was able to pick up the target, and it achieved superior results. Another flight picked up another target and bombed it. This was the town of Krimm, with its important marshalling yard and highway, which were severely damaged. A third flight hit the town of Kronen-Burgerhutte. Moderate to intense heavy flak followed the formation from bomb-line to the target area and knocked down two aeroplanes from the 669th BS. The formation suffered heavy flak damage on this mission.'

The second 669th aircraft to be lost was the A-26 flown by Lt Kehoe, his bomber being downed in flames over the target. While a number of Invader crews observed enemy fighters during the course of the mission, the fighter escort prevented them from attacking the bombers. Many of the A-26s returned to Melun intact but badly riddled by flak.

The 416th's second mission of the day saw it target the defended village of Hillsheim. As usual the Invaders were led by glazed-nose A-20Js. The following account is also taken from the 668th BS official history;

'At just after 1400 hrs the next mission was already taking off. This was group mission number 177, and it was to strike us a hard blow. We had nine crews take part from this squadron, two of them leading both boxes. Capt "Rick" Prentiss, with Lt Burseil and gunners Brown and Wylie, led the first box in an A-20J. Right behind them, leading the second box, was Maj Price with Lt Hand and gunner Fild at the 0.50-cals. This was Fild's 51st mission, and upon return he was due to head home. These are the twists of fate that cut deep. The target was the defended village of Hillsheim. Again, all of this bombing was done to put a crimp in von Runstedt's drive. The flight over was quiet till the target area was reached, then all hell broke loose, the effects – devastation. Rick Prentiss rocked his aeroplane all over the sky in evasive action but to no avail. The flak was heavy and intense and clawed at the aeroplanes in the sky. Bursts of flak surrounded Prentiss' aeroplane, and also caught his wingman and deputy. Both were seen to go down with no 'chutes blossoming. They crashed and no one escaped to the knowledge of the eyewitnesses.'

The squadron history added that Capt Prentiss was to be married in three months' time. It goes on;

'The rest of the formation made it back to base after dropping their loads. They were very battered and broken up, and both Maj Price and Lt "Buck" Buchanan couldn't bring their aeroplanes back to the dispersal area – they had to be towed back. The flight lasted three hours, and all the aeroplanes bore evidence of flak. It was dusk as the last bomber landed, signalling the end of the day.'

Another A-26 from the 669th was also forced down, but its crew returned later, safe and sound.

On 26 December the group attempted two missions, one in the morning and the other in the afternoon. Both were recalled as the fighter escort did not make the rendezvous. Early the next day the men of the 416th had an experience that proved to be unique for them. The incident is best described by the 668th BS history, which states;

'At 0100 hrs we received an air raid alert on the field. In the bitter cold everyone piled into their foxholes. For 30 minutes nothing occurred and the "all clear" was sounded. Everyone crawled back into the sack for a good rest. Five minutes later the roar of machine guns and cannon filled the air. In nothing flat the tents cleared, no one waiting for the siren. GIs were sitting in their foxholes, some in only their underwear. The field received a good strafe job by what was believed to be a Ju 88. It lasted for ten minutes and then the "all clear" was sounded again. It was discovered that someone had set a flare in a nearby field and guided the aeroplane in. That was the information we received from a higher source. Luckily there was no damage and no one was injured. This was the first strafe job in the squadron's career. Needless to say, it had a remarkable effect on us.'

At 1100 hrs on 27 December 29 aircraft took off on the group's 178th mission, their target being the railway bridge at Eller, spanning the Moselle River. It had been assigned to the group the day before but not bombed as the formation had been recalled due to a lack of fighter escort. This time the group dropped a total of 87 1000-lb and 26 500-lb bombs. All aircraft returned 3 hrs and 30 min later with no losses, casualties or battle damage. The bombing results were rated as excellent to superior, with the ordnance having blanketed the bridge. The structure still stood, however, although it had been rendered unserviceable.

Bad weather on the 28th prevented the group flying any missions, but the next day it was sent to bomb the road bridge at Keuchingen. When the 34 aircraft arrived over the target crews found it obscured by the weather. Two attempts were made to sight and bomb the bridge, but to no avail. The aircraft retained their ordnance and returned to base, landing safely after a mission lasting 3 hrs 20 min.

The weather prevented any missions on 30 and 31 December too, although conditions began to clear in the late afternoon of New Year's Eve, but too late for an operation to be flown. The improving weather produced an equally clear moonlit night, which almost proved disastrous for the group. At midnight the air was filled with the sounds of small arms fire as personnel celebrated the New Year. This activity may well have proved beneficial for the men of the 416th, but not in a manner they might have expected. Approximately 20 minutes later a Ju 88 attacked Melun, taking advantage of the bright moonlit night. When the air raid alert was sounded those personnel already awake quickly reached their foxholes, and safety. Despite the benefit of the moonlight the German bombardier's aim was poor and his bombs missed the airfield. But they did hit the railway station at Coubert, three miles north of the field, and a road near the village of Lissy was strafed. The attack had a sobering effect on the numerous small celebrations being held around the base. The anti-aircraft guns surrounding Melun fired at the Ju 88 but it was not hit and made good its escape.

The incident kept many of the group's personnel awake, or sleeping lightly, ready to respond to another visit by the Luftwaffe. They spent much of New Year's Day 1945 enlarging and deepening their foxholes.

As 1944 drew to a close, the Ninth Bombardment Division issued the following press release detailing the operations conducted by its medium bomber units in the wake of the German Ardennes counteroffensive;

'News reports continued to emphasise the seriousness of the German counteroffensive on the Western front, but fog-covered battle areas kept the B-26s, A-20s and A-26s of the Ninth Bombardment Division tied to the ground. The airmen wanted to help the footsloggers who were reeling backward under the weight of von Rundstedt's counter attack. They were eager to give support like that at Cherbourg, Caen, St Lo, Falaise and the Rouen loop. Now, if ever, was the time when tactical air power was needed. But the weather favoured the enemy, whose counter attack, launched on 16 December, in a blanket of fog, had punched swiftly into western Belgium under soupy skies. For seven days airmen "sweated out" a break in the weather. Then, on 23 December, the skies cleared over the snow-swept frontlines, allowing air support to go to the rescue of embattled Allied ground forces.

'Maj Gen Samuel E Anderson, commanding the Ninth Bombardment Division, put 657 medium bombers over the western front on the first clear weather day, despatching Marauders, Havocs and Invaders to attack bridges, road junctions and villages within the communications network supplying the German counteroffensive.

'Determination of crewmen to aid ground forces was so great that one group elected to carry out its attack without fighter escort rather than abandon its mission. The group was jumped by more than 75 ME 109s and FW 190s but completed its attack, despite the loss of 16 bombers out of a formation of 36. German fighters jumped four groups in all, as the division engaged in its biggest aerial battle with the Luftwaffe. Some 32 enemy fighters were shot down, 12 probably destroyed and 33 more reported damaged, at a cost of 36 bombers.

'The weather, which earlier in the month had been so much in the enemy's favour, now had turned against him. For five days, from 23 to

27 December, Marauders, Havocs and Invaders, flying 2554 sorties, struck at communications centres, bridges, defended villages and other strong points within or immediately behind the central sector of the western front where the counter attack had been launched.

'Coming as it did at the fag end of December, the five-day aerial assault provided a smashing climax to a year's operations for the division.

This aircraft was damaged beyond repair by a lone night intruder that attacked Melun during December 1944

Not a big month as bombing figures go, December, however, saw the medium bombers again delivering the punch that months before had made them famous in paving the way for the invasion and sealing off the Normandy battle area to enemy troop and supply movements.'

FIRST MISSION OF 1945

The group flew its first mission of 1945 on the morning of 1 January when the 416th pioneered a new type of attack, but with little success. Six aeroplanes were despatched from the 670th BS (one A-20J and five A-26s) to bomb the command post and corps HQ at Mont-le-Ban from a medium altitude. They were then to descend to deck level and strafe the target if the flak encountered was not too intense. All the aircraft were equipped with wing guns for this mission, boosting the bombers' individual armament to 14 fixed 0.50-in machine guns.

The formation made three runs on the target at 8000 ft amidst an intense heavy flak barrage from the 28 heavy guns at Houffalise, close to the target. The first pass was an observation run only, and on the second run the bombardier could not align his bombsight with the target as his A-20J was too close to the aim point when escorting fighter-bombers dropped their smoke bombs. By the time the flight made its third pass the smoke from the latter had disappeared. The A-26 flown by Lt Murphy jettisoned its bombs in the target area and was last seen going down over enemy territory. Four other aircraft received battle damage, but the crews returned safely. No strafing was attempted due to the intense flak.

The following day, as crews were briefing at 0730 hrs for an attack on the railway bridge at Simmern, in Germany, a ground haze moved into the area. Despite conditions being very foggy at ground level, above the fog the sky was clear. Nevertheless, crews experienced problems with the weather before the aircraft had taken off, as the heavy mist froze onto the windscreens of many of the Invaders as they taxied out. This severely restricted the visibility for a number of the pilots. Indeed, the mist was so thick that it was impossible to see the A-26s from the control tower.

One of those that managed to take off was Lt Harris, although his aircraft developed engine trouble soon after he had left Melun and he was forced to return to base. He had company, as Lt Montrose's aircraft was also stricken by engine problems and forced to abort the mission as well. Lt Roberts' Invader suffered a double engine failure just as he took off, leaving him no choice but to make an immediate forced landing straight ahead and at the very end of the runway. Upon landing the aircraft rolled

This is the A-26B of Lt Roberts and Sgt Windisch that crashed on take-off at Melun on 2 January 1945. Acting swiftly, Windisch rescued Roberts from the wreckage and pulled him behind a tree just moments before their aircraft exploded and burned out

This 668th BS aircraft also crashed on take-off on 2 January 1945 as a result of icy weather conditions. In this case, both Lt Lackner and his gunner, Cpl Mussarra, escaped uninjured. Note that the gunner's canopy is covered in frost

out in to the fields and both engines caught fire. Acting quickly, gunner Sgt Windisch pulled Roberts out of the cockpit of the bomber. Seeking cover, both men ran to the trees, reaching them just as the Invader's bomb load exploded and scattered bits of A-26 all over the immediate area.

When the aircraft exploded the men of the 416th, believing the field was again under attack, dived into the nearest foxhole. The concussion of the explosion blew Roberts from the tree behind which he was sheltering and sent him sliding across a frozen pond! He was uninjured nevertheless.

Just as Lt Lackner became airborne both his engines quit too and his aircraft came down in a similar manner to that of Roberts', although the Invader did not explode. Lackner and his gunner, Cpl Mussarra, were able to walk away from the wreck, but Lt Clark's aircraft from the 669th BS did not fare so well because his A-26 exploded when it too crashed shortly after take-off. Both he and his gunner perished. A subsequent investigation of the crashed machine revealed that ice forming on the wings of the aircraft had been responsible for it spinning in.

Despite these accidents at the start of the mission, the rest of the group reached the target without further incident. The attack on the bridge was accomplished from altitudes of 11,600 ft up to 12,000 ft, and although enemy fighters were seen, no flak was encountered. Bombing results were rated as excellent to superior, but the bridge itself remained standing despite miles of track and structures in front of and behind it having been destroyed. The Allies desperately wanted the target neutralised as it was the only bridge open at that time in this area for transport heading southwest from Koblenz and Mainz to the frontline.

The group returned to Simmern on 5 January for another attempt at destroying the bridge, but as the weather was still bad it was decided to use PFF bombing methods instead. A PFF-equipped Marauder led each of the two boxes of A-26s from the 416th BG, and as expected the crews found the target to be completely covered by cloud. Both boxes dropped their bombs upon receiving a signal from the PFF Marauders. The cloud cover also prevented the results from being assessed, and the bombers returned to their base at dusk after a four-hour mission.

It was 11 January before the weather permitted the group to fly another mission, which was again led by PFF B-26s. The bridge at Simmern was the target, and by now some of the 28 crews from the 416th that were sent to attack it must have been wondering if it had become their own private target! The PFF aircraft suffered equipment failure over the bridge

so the pathfinder bombardier attacked a secondary target – railway tracks near Alsey – and the Invaders dropped on his lead.

Two days later the next mission was flown in temperatures that had plummeted to well below freezing. Lt Roberts' jinx struck once again, for as he and his gunner, Sgt Windesen, cleared the runway their aircraft settled back to the ground and crash-landed. This time, however, the A-26 did not explode. Minutes later Lt Nathanson and his gunner were forced to return to base when the nose gear of their A-26 refused to retract. The remaining 22 group aircraft (including a PFF B-26) reached the target – a bridge at Steinbruck, near the German-Belgian border – and bombed it by PFF. There was no flak, and no fighters were encountered at the target to hamper their bomb runs. The aim of the PFF Marauder was off target, however, so the following A-26 crews that bombed as briefed upon receiving a signal from the B-26 saw their ordnance fall short of the target. The mission results were duly classified as 'poor'. Upon returning to Melun, the group found its base weathered in, and crews were forced to land and stay overnight at Laon. The group suffered no losses, damage or casualties during the mission.

On 14 January the aircraft that had not flown on the previous day's operation were prepared for a PFF-led attack on the communications centre at Schleiden. Departing from a snow-capped runway, the first A-26 to take off (from the 660th BS) mushed in on take-off and exploded, killing both crew members. The probable cause of the crash was again excessive wing and carburettor icing – an issue that plagued both Allied and Axis aircraft in the ETO during the winter.

The bombers encountered little flak over the target, and bombs were dropped from 13,000 ft once the A-26s had received the signal from the PFF Marauder. The bombing results were rated as excellent after a review of post-strike photographs. While the mission was in progress the aircraft that had been forced to land at A69 the day before returned to Melun. Ironically, their place was taken by a number of returning crews from the Schleiden raid after they also found Melun to be weathered in. On this occasion the recoveries were more eventful, with the A-26 flown by Lt Cannon crashing on landing due to a faulty undercarriage. Lt Blevins also experienced landing gear problems and crash-landed as well. Both crews were picked up from A69 by the 416th BG's C-64 hack aircraft and returned safely to Melun. The rest of the formation landed at A58 Coulommiers and returned to Melun at dusk.

The following day the 416th was the only group in the Ninth Bombardment Division to fly a mission due to thick cloud cover. Once again the target was the bridge at Simmern, and 45 crews were briefed to attack it. On each of the previous attempts to destroy the bridge the approaches at either end had been hit, but the structure itself remained intact and undamaged. En route to the target no flak was encountered, and the group bombed using the British navigational aid *Gee*. The latter enabled an aircraft to accurately fix its position by measuring the relative time required for pulses of radio energy to travel from three ground stations to the bomber. A total of 50,000 lbs of bombs were unloaded on the target but the cloud cover meant that the results of the attack had to be categorised as undetermined. The mission lasted for more than four hours, and all aircraft and crews returned safely to Melun.

On 16 January the target was another railway bridge, this time at Sinzig. In the afternoon two A-20Ks led two flights totalling 37 A-26s – sufficient numbers of glazed-nose A-26Cs, or field kits to allow the group to use them to lead all of its missions, were still unavailable. Pending the arrival of more C-models, both A-20s and B-26s would be used to lead the attacks, as well as to act as 'window' aircraft. The latter would drop several thousand slivers of tin strips per bomber near the target area, thus causing false returns on enemy radar screens. An advanced form of it remains in use today as a countermeasure against radar and missiles, but it is now known as 'chaff'.

En route to the target the group encountered weak but fairly accurate flak, and once crews were over the bridge itself this developed into moderate to heavy, accurate, flak. Bombing was accomplished from altitudes up to 13,700 ft, and a review of post-strike photographs rated the results as excellent. Several aircraft sustained flak damage but all returned to Melun and landed safely after 3 hrs and 35 min in the air.

The ever-present bad weather kept the 416th BG on the ground until 21 January, when the target was the railway bridge at Euskirchen – an important link in the supply route between Cologne and the frontline. B-26 groups had previously hit the target on 23 December, knocking out all five railway lines that crossed the bridge, but the Germans had since repaired one of them. An A-20J flew ahead of the A-26s and dropped 'window'. But despite the latter the attackers still encountered moderate but accurate flak when they reached the target and as they turned away after releasing their bombs. Twelve aircraft were damaged, and the bombing was accomplished with precision from 12,000 ft. No flak or fighters were encountered after leaving the target and all aircraft landed safely at Melun. A review of post-mission photos showed bombing results ranging from undetermined to excellent and superior. Extensive damage was done to the bridge, tracks and a nearby marshalling yard.

On the morning of 22 January, the 416th flew the first of two missions assigned to it that day. The group sent 33 aircraft to attack the Simmern bridge once again and, as before, the target area was completely obscured by bad weather. This was a PFF mission, and the group also sent three of its A-20Js to drop 'window'. Weak flak was encountered during the flight to the target but none once over the bridge itself. Nevertheless, one aircraft was hit by flak and sustained minor damage. The first box of Invaders bombed on receiving the signal from the PFF Marauder leading the group. The second box elected to bomb on ETA – that is, they dropped their bombs at their estimated time of arrival over the target. The ordnance was salvoed from an altitude of 12,500 ft, but as the target was obscured by heavy clouds the results were unobserved.

While the 416th was heading for Simmern other Ninth Air Force bomber and fighter-bomber groups attacked the bridge at Dasburg, completely destroying it. This resulted in some 1500 German vehicles being stranded nose to tail as they attempted to flee eastward away from advancing Allied forces. An alert liaison aircraft pilot spotted the traffic jam and called for artillery fire on the concentration of vehicles. He also requested that aircraft be sent to attack them, and six A-26s from the 416th BG were hastily despatched to strafe the stranded convoy that was jammed around both ends of the bridge. However, poor weather over the target area and the lack of a fighter escort meant that all the aircraft were subsequently recalled.

Even though it was aborted, this mission represented a milestone for USAAF medium and light bomb groups in the ETO because it was the first time that they had been given permission to attack a target at low-level (below 1000 ft) since the disastrous Ijmuiden power station raid of 17 May 1943. The latter mission had seen the 322nd BG

send ten B-26s to attack targets in the Dutch town, aircraft flying at less than 100 ft for the duration of the operation. The group had bombed Ijmuiden just 72 hours earlier, and for reasons still not fully explained, the follow-up attack saw the USAAF aircraft flying the same route to the target as before. It was not that attacking the same target was an error, as multiple raids were often required to achieve the desired outcome, but it was not advisable to use the same timing, route and altitude because the enemy would be ready. Consequently, the attacking aircraft would be on the receiving end of a very nasty, and possibly disastrous, surprise. This is precisely what happened when the 322nd BG returned to Ijmuiden.

The flak batteries and fighters were waiting for the B-26s, and all ten were shot down – the last one ditched into the sea just after crossing the Dutch coast. The anti-aircraft guns were heavily concentrated around German military positions, making low-level attacks by bombers extremely hazardous. In the wake of this disastrous mission, US medium bombers in the ETO were restricted from flying low-level sorties over enemy territory. However, following the arrival of the appreciably quicker A-26, this restriction was removed because these aircraft had been designed and built precisely for this type of mission. The Allies had also achieved air superiority in Europe by late 1944.

The Invader at last got the chance to prove its worth at low-level in the ETO on 23 January when the 416th flew bombing and strafing missions against vehicle and troop concentrations at Blankenheim and Dasburg. Despite poor weather conditions, the group sent six A-26s from the 670th BS to attack a convoy in Dasburg, but only one of the crews was able to locate the target and bomb it from 3000 ft, before descending to the deck and making a strafing pass. The other five were unable to acquire the target visually and did not attack. The flak, however, was heavy and accurate, and two A-26s were hit, although they were able to make successful crash landings in friendly territory.

One of the aircraft struck by flak was the A-26 flown by veteran pilot Capt Paul Atkinson. He had lost sight of the formation in the poor weather conditions soon after take-off, although he did make radio contact with it. As he arrived over the target Atkinson encountered heavy and accurate flak which hit his aircraft, badly damaging its left engine. The pilot immediately shut it down and feathered the propeller. Shrapnel had also hit Atkinson's bombardier/navigator, Lt Dale Ackerson, in the left leg, almost severing it at the ankle. The cockpit was filling with smoke

This A-26B crashed in wintry conditions whilst landing at Melun after a training flight. The crew escaped without injury

Yet another landing gear collapse inflicted this damage to a clamshell canopy A-26 in early 1945. Note the wooden trestle beneath the bomber's nose

from the damaged engine, so Atkinson released the canopy escape hatch. Flak had also damaged the elevator controls, rendering them useless, but the elevator trim tab still functioned. By using it, Atkinson was able to retain some control over the aircraft. The bombs were dropped over the target area to lighten the aircraft, and as a safety measure in case of a crash landing.

Both Atkinson and Ackerson felt the A-26 vibrating and thought that their gunner, SSgt Collier, was firing the turret guns. When the smoke had cleared from the cockpit, Atkinson used the elevator trim tab to lower the nose and fire the nose guns.

When the aircraft was hit by flak, Atkinson continued to fly the same course while he regained control. Since the A-26 was heading away from A55, the pilot reversed his course and again fired his nose guns. Despite his wounds causing him severe pain and rapid blood loss, Ackerson continued to plot their position and provide course corrections to the pilot. Atkinson noticed that the red jettison indicator light was on, which indicated that Collier had probably bailed out. While trying to staunch the bleeding wound in his leg, Ackerson continued to navigate and provide Atkinson with updated headings and course changes. The pilot made three attempts to radio for fighter protection but got no response.

The right engine was running at full throttle and the severely damaged aircraft was travelling at 240 mph on one engine. As it passed the target area the A-26 took another flak hit, wounding Ackerson in the right leg above the ankle. Although the last hit had damaged the cockpit instruments and destroyed the airspeed indicator, the pilot was still able to fly his stricken bomber.

Once over friendly territory, Atkinson realised that his bombardier/navigator was in danger of bleeding to death, so he decided to land as soon as possible to save Ackerson's life. Picking out a small field, Atkinson crash-landed with the flaps down on ground that sloped upwards. The mortally damaged A-26 slid across the field, passing a tree on the crest before coming to a brutally sudden stop in a gully. Ackerson was thrown out, dislocating his shoulder on landing in the snow. Atkinson had locked his shoulder harness and lap belt just before setting the aircraft down, causing him to be trapped in the aircraft for several minutes. Fortunately for him there was no fire, and US infantrymen were soon on the scene.

While several of the soldiers released Atkinson, others gave Ackerson first aid. Both men were rushed to the closest field hospital, where it was discovered that Atkinson had suffered a fractured ankle and wrist during the crash-landing. It was determined that SSgt Collier had probably bailed out when he saw the jettisoned canopy go past his station. This was the 'last resort' signal to bail out in case the interphone, emergency bell and gunner's call light had been knocked out. Collier was listed by the 416th BG as missing in action. Both Atkinson and Ackerson were transferred to a general hospital for further treatment.

Lt Theron S Merritt, who was in Capt Atkinson's flight, was also unable to stay in formation due to the bad weather. He descended from 8000 ft to about 1000 ft to strafe some German vehicles he had found concealed in a town in the area. Coming upon a second town, he released his bombs on another concentration of vehicles. Light flak was directed at his aircraft and SSgt Raymond J Gatti strafed the gun emplacements with his lower turret guns. Because Merritt executed violent evasive action, the flak gunners managed to put only two small holes in his aircraft. Unable to locate the rest of his flight, he proceeded to A68 and landed safely.

Shortly after noon it was the 671st BS's turn to send out six A-26s on bombing and strafing attacks. Soon after take-off, Lt J C Gary found that he was unable to retract his landing gear. He flew a tight circuit in his heavy Invader and stalled in just above the runway, causing the undercarriage to collapse and the aircraft to career off into rough ground with a full load of bombs and ammunition aboard. Fortunately for Gary and his gunner, SSgt R W Cheuvront, the A-26 did not explode and they escaped without injury.

Due to the adverse weather the remaining five Invaders had difficulty locating each other and forming up. After take-off, Flt Off H J Wilson (who had crash-landed at the end of his first mission just over a week earlier) lost sight of the formation when it passed through cloud cover. Two other A-26s also became separated and were unable to find a suitable target, so they returned to Melun. Leading the remaining aircraft, Capt R J Tutt found the target and began his bomb run. Flak was heavy and accurate, making it impossible to maintain tight formation at the briefed bombing altitude. Tutt's aircraft was struck several times, and the hits knocked out the hydraulic system and the VHF radio set. Bombardier/navigator Lt J T Beck was wounded in the foot.

Unable to bomb due to the severe flak damage, and with his bombardier/navigator wounded, Tutt immediately pulled away from the target. Despite his painful injuries, Beck was able to provide Tutt with course headings to A69, where they made an emergency crash-landing. Emergency crews rushed to the damaged A-26 and removed Beck for prompt medical treatment.

Only Capt L C Nielson managed to bomb a target near Berk, but not before he too had been wounded by shrapnel that broke his canopy and lacerated his face with Plexiglas splinters. The hit also destroyed his gunsight. Nielson was knocked out by the impact, and when he regained consciousness he found that he was diving through 1000 ft out of control. He quickly recovered the aircraft, and despite painful wounds and Plexiglas splinters in his eyes, Nielson pressed on with the mission. Flak was encountered but there were no further hits. He sighted and bombed a column of German vehicles in the town of Berk. After his attack he proceeded to A68 Juvincourt, where he landed without further incident.

Meanwhile, flying alone, Flt Off Wilson and his gunner, Sgt V S Stypenski, found and attacked the railway junction near Blankenheim from a height of 3000 ft. After the mission Wilson reported;

'I missed the formation, but rather than turn back, I continued on course to the target. When I reached Blankenheim there were A-20s strafing the road, so I circled about until they pulled away, then peeled off, dropped frags (bombs) at 500 ft and went down on the deck. I then

Although boasting impressive nose art, as well as a growing bomb tally, the identity of this A-26B from the 416th BG remains a mystery . . .

proceeded to strafe vehicles and soldiers along the road, one truck veering off the road and piling into a ditch with black smoke pouring from it.'

Having destroyed one large truck and damaged three more, Wilson's A-26 was then hit by ground fire in the right wing and the left engine, the latter suffering a hole in an oil line. Despite damage to the aircraft, neither crewman was wounded. Wilson was able to make a safe landing at Juvincourt. Two other 671st BS pilots, Lt A E Herman and Lt T J Murray, were unable to bomb or strafe due to poor weather. Indeed, only three of the 12 A-26s sent out that day by the 416th BG successfully attacked the assigned target. The official squadron history of the 671st BS made the following comment about the mission;

'All men of the flight were taken in to Bomber Division immediately for a consultation with Gen Anderson. The general seemed satisfied with the comments of the group, and personally commended Capt Nielson and Flt Off Wilson for their extraordinary achievements.'

The senior officer referred to was the same Maj Gen Samuel E Anderson mentioned by Lt Col Hankey in his account of the arrival of the Project Squadron at Great Dunmow (see Chapter One). All the crews from the latter unit were assigned to the 416th BG after they had helped the group convert to the A-26. The Project Squadron CO was posted to group operations, while his pilots were assigned to the 670th BS. It therefore appears that Gen Anderson held a different opinion of the quality of the pilots and crews to that expressed by Hankey.

The communications centre and road junction at Schleiden was the target on 24 January. Unlike the missions flown during the previous 48 hours, this was to be a routine medium altitude attack. The group sent 15 A-26s and six bombardier-carrying A-20s, with three of the latter also carrying 'window' to confuse German radar and reduce the effectiveness of the anti-aircraft barrage. The flak over the target was reported as light and inaccurate, and none of the aircraft were damaged. Bombing was accomplished visually, with 500-lb bombs being dropped from 12,000 ft. Over the target, only two of the three flights were able to release their bombs, and the results were rated as excellent. The bombsight in the lead A-20 of the third flight malfunctioned due to a broken telescopic cable, forcing the aircraft to return to base with their bombs still aboard.

. . . as does the identity of this lead ship A-26C

1ST LT. G. W. PETERSON

The following day the group attacked the communications centre at Kall. This was the 416th's fifth mission in seven days, and as with the other medium level strikes, it saw A-20s leading the A-26s to the target. A 'window'-carrying Havoc again preceded the formation in an effort to disrupt the enemy radar and flak batteries, but on this particular occasion neither flak nor fighters were encountered by the bombers.

The crews reported that the exploding bombs appeared to chase a small German convoy along the road leading into town. They also stated that after the bombing, the vehicles had disappeared in a blanket of smoke. The bombs completely blanketed the road junction, damaging buildings, the railway line and the road. A siding with 20 wagons filled with supplies was also destroyed. The bombing results for all flights bar one were rated as excellent to superior, but those of the flight led by Capt G M McNulty were rated as unsatisfactory. As the bombardier, Lt Forma, opened the bomb-bay doors the ordnance immediately and inexplicably fell out of the A-20's bomb-bay. As this was the signal for the following A-26s to release, all the bombs dropped by the flight fell well short of the target.

On the 26th the weather deteriorated further, preventing any flying at all, let alone combat missions, until the 29th when it cleared enough to enable the group to fly a morning mission against the road bridge at Nonnweiler. This was the group's last mission of the month, and as bad weather had so often plagued its operations for several months, it was expected that the target would be obscured. Crews were therefore briefed to fly it as a PFF mission to allow for that contingency. Three aircraft were sent to release 'window' to ensure some safety from flak over the target.

The 416th had been concentrating on road bridges and crossroads since Christmas, as those targets had been assigned top priority when it came to disrupting the enemy. When crews arrived over the target, they found it completely obscured as anticipated. They bombed on signal from the PFF Marauder, the A-26s dropping 1000-lb general purpose (GP) bombs and the A-20s 500-lb GPs from 13,000 ft. The cloud cover over the target prevented observation of the results, but the mission was flown without interference from flak or fighters and all aircraft returned to Melun with no damage or casualties.

The weather was again bad on 30 and 31 January, so no further missions were flown until 1 February, when the group's target was the defended village of Schleiden. The group had originally briefed enough crews and prepared sufficient aircraft to make up the usual two boxes of A-26s, but just as the pilots were preparing to 'start engines', Group Operations decided to remove the entire second box. This had comprised 11 Invaders and one 'window'-carrying A-20 of the 668th BS. The order did not include the single Havoc, however, which therefore became the only aircraft from that squadron to participate in the mission.

Four Invaders from the 669th BS/ 416th BG head for Germany in good weather conditions in early 1945

As a low ceiling was forecast, the mission was led by a PFF-equipped Marauder. On its signal all the aircraft bombed through the overcast from 12,500 ft, the cloud cover preventing both visual observation of the results and post-strike photo-reconnaissance of the target area. After a total mission time of three hours, all aircraft safely returned to Melun without battle damage or casualties.

The next day's mission was an attack on the communications centre at Euskirchen, which was also being used as a supply depot as well as providing accommodation for German troops being sent to the frontline. The group encountered heavy and accurate flak over the target, and two A-26s were shot down. One was hit in the wing, which broke away from the fuselage, and the aircraft was last seen in an uncontrollable spin at 5000 ft. No parachutes were observed leaving the doomed bomber. The other A-26 was hit hard by flak, but its crew was able to bail out safely.

Weather over the target was clear and the group bombed from 12,500 ft, with results being observed and reported as excellent. Strike photography confirmed that the results for four of the six flights were indeed excellent. Due to extreme evasive action necessary to avoid flak, the other two flights were unable to take strike photographs. Each of the surviving A-26s sustained flak damage, but they were able to return to Melun and land safely. A solitary 'window' A-20 was also badly shot up, with one gunner being killed and the other bailing out over Germany. The pilot managed to crash-land the Havoc in friendly territory.

The 3 February mission gave the 668th BS crews a sense of déjà vu, as once again orders called for two boxes from the group but the entire second box, comprising aircraft from the squadron, was pulled from the mission except for the 'window'-carrying A-20. The objective was the storage and repair depot at Berg/Gladbach. Cloud cover over the target was anticipated and a PFF-equipped Marauder led the group. Bombing was from 13,500 ft and the results were rated as 'uncharacterised' due to the cloud cover. Light flak was encountered over the target, but it caused very little damage to the attacking aircraft, all of which returned and landed safely at Melun.

No mission was flown by the group the next day as it was preparing to move to its new base at A69 Laon, 65 miles northeast of Paris – it had previously been occupied by the B-26-equipped 323rd BG, which would in turn move to A83 Denain on 9 February. A55 would subsequently be assigned to Troop Carrier Command. An advanced element of personnel left Melun by truck on the morning of the 5th and arrived there in the middle of the night. The following morning they began setting up tents and performing other tasks necessary to prepare for the arrival of the remainder of the group. Meanwhile, the air echelon continued to fly combat missions from Melun on the 6th, 8th, 9th and 10th.

On the 6th motor transport and armoured vehicles were attacked at Berg/Gladbach, and although the target was obscured by weather, bombs were released on a signal from the leading PFF Marauder. Visual observation and strike photography was rendered impossible by the cloud cover. No flak or fighters were encountered, but Melun was closed due to weather, the returning aircraft diverting to the new airfield at Laon, where they landed safely. No mission was flown on the 7th, allowing the aircraft that had diverted to Laon the day before to return to Melun.

The hardworking groundcrew of A-26B *DENVER DARLING* from the 416th BG pose for the camera in front of their aircraft

INVADERS TO THE FORE

The 416th BG reached a significant milestone on 8 February 1945. Not only was the day's mission the first to be flown entirely with the A-26, it was also the unit's 200th operation in the ETO. The group had achieved this total in less than a year, flying its first mission on 3 March 1944. It had now received enough C-model Invaders to be able to use them to lead A-26Bs. The remaining A-20s could now be retired.

The mission, led by 671st BS CO Lt Col D L Willetts, was intended to support ground units that would shortly be passing through the target area – the defended town of Nutterden. However, it was obscured by the weather and the group dropped its bombs using the *Gee* system on the town of Elton instead. The weather also prevented visual observation and strike photography of the bombing results. All but one of the attacking aircraft returned to Melun and landed safely. When just 12 miles from home an A-26 ran out fuel and crashed, Lt Steed of the 669th BG being killed and his unnamed gunner surviving with serious injuries.

The next day's target was the communications centre at Kempen, which lay in the path of the advancing British Second Army at the northern end of the 'Siegfried Line'. Shortly after take-off Lt Nathanson was forced to abort the mission when one of his engines overheated. The ever-present bad weather went one step beyond the usual veiling of the target and completely covered the area to the extent that the entire group lost its way. Most crews therefore proceeded to attack secondary targets, although Capt R E Greenley of the 671st BS, flying with bombardier/navigator Lt R J Basnett and gunner SSgt J H Migues, succeeded in attacking Kempen. Greenley was one of the few remaining pilots who had come across with the 671st BS in early 1944. He became flight leader in early July and was promoted to captain prior to flying his final mission. Greenley flew his last six missions with Lt Basnett as his bombardier.

Lt Lou Prucha's A-26B-20-DL 41-39274 *Sugar Baby* of the 668th BS taxis along the perimeter track at Melun with other 416th BG A-26s prior to flying a mission in early 1945. The groundcrew has just started to apply the name and artwork to the nose of the aircraft

Once completed the artwork featured a baby dropping a bomb, as well as the *Sugar Baby* titling

Two 668th BS A-26s were forced to make emergency landings after running out of fuel, Lt Cannon coming down in a field in Holland. Although his aircraft was considerably damaged, both he and his gunner, SSgt Holland, were uninjured. Lt Montrose had just enough fuel to allow him time find the new field at Laon and land safely. The rest of the group returned to Melun, where they all landed without incident.

The target for the 10th was the truck repair depot at Bad Münstereifel (which had been attacked by the 416th on Christmas Day), and cloud cover again meant that it was a PFF-led mission. Light but inaccurate flak was reported over the target. The 668th BS history states that since the bombing was accomplished by PFF no strike photos were taken.

The 416th BG also commenced a base move on 10 February, with the majority of the ground echelon having left Melun the previous afternoon as the following extract from the 669th BS history explains;

'During the afternoon of the 9th the train echelon left. This consisted of most of the squadron personnel. The boys were loaded into vehicles of all kinds and were transported to Melun, where they boarded the train. From the beginning it was rough, as the train consisted of the "famed" 40 x 8s. These contrivances are nothing more than small boxcars, cold and very uncomfortable. They hold either 40 men or eight horses. This train convoy left at roughly 0800 hrs.'

The rest of the group's personnel left at 0130 hrs the next morning, and arrived at Laon at 1000 hrs. In order to keep the group operational during this time the aircrews, crew chief and armament personnel were to fly to Laon at a later date. The move was completed on 12 February and the first mission from the new base was scheduled for the following day. The histories of the 669th and 671st BSs contain brief entries for missions after the first week of February, while those of the other two squadrons barely mention the missions much beyond the essential information.

The target for 13 February was the motor transport depot at Iserlohn, the 668th BS history stating, 'The primary target was not bombed for some reason and the secondary target at Wittlich was attacked instead. Bombing was done using *Gee*, and the results are not known due to cloud cover. All aeroplanes returned safely to base after a trip of 2 hr 30 min duration'. According to the 670th BS history, 'Seven of our crews took part. No photo cover was available, so the results were unobserved'.

On 14 February the crews of the 416th flew two missions as the Ninth Bombardment Division enjoyed its most active day since 25 December 1944 in terms of sorties generated. The group's target in the morning was the truck depot in the town of Mechernich, and as its aircraft were leaving the target they encountered heavy and accurate flak. The aircraft of Lt Chalmers from the 670th BS was hit and it dropped out of the formation. Burning heavily, the Invader was observed falling away out of control. The other crews reported seeing a parachute, which gave hope that someone was able to get out. No other parachutes were seen.

All remaining aircraft in the formation sustained damage ranging from light to heavy. Lt Babbage, who was Capt Anderson's bombardier/navigator, was extremely fortunate for as he was bending over the bombsight, a piece of shrapnel entered the aircraft's nose and passed through the other side of the fuselage. Had he not been bent over his sight, Babbage would have been hit and possibly killed.

Bombing was accomplished by PFF and the results were unobserved by the formation. Post-strike photo-reconnaissance showed damaged railway lines, as well as buildings and cars that had been damaged and burned out. Apart from Chalmers' A-26, all other aircraft returned safely.

The afternoon mission was an attack on the ammunition dump at Rheinbach, ten miles southwest of Bonn. There was little flak over the target and the skies were clear of the clouds that quite often prevented visual bombing of targets – a pathfinder had been sent nevertheless, but it was unable to rendezvous with the A-26s. Crews were instructed to attack visually, and as they closed their bomb-bay doors and began to leave the target area, they were able to observe the impact of their bombs. Direct hits were scored on the target, and crews reported seeing enormous explosions, brilliant flames and smoke reaching high into the sky as the ammunition dump was totally destroyed. Bombing results were rated as superior. There were no losses, with all aircraft landing safely at Laon at dusk.

The target for 16 February was the ordnance depot at Unna, in the heavily defended Ruhr Valley. Targets such as this were usually attacked by high-flying B-17s and B-24s from the Eighth Air Force, but they were busy that day supporting the Soviet Red Army's advance on Berlin. The Ninth Bombardment Division aircraft attacked from just 12,000 ft, although it was hoped that poor weather conditions would save the B-26s and A-26s from the worst of the flak. The results of the mission were not recorded by any of the squadrons, and the histories of the 668th and 670th BSs differ about the level of flak encountered, that of the 668th stating that 'no flak harassed the formation, which returned after 3 hrs 30 min'. On the other hand the 670th history states that 'the Unna ordnance depot was hit with undetermined results on 16 February. Eight 670 crews took part. Moderate to intense heavy accurate flak was met at the target and the turn-off. One aeroplane from the formation went down'.

There is no mention of any losses suffered by the other three squadrons for that mission. The reason for the discrepancy is unknown, but during war conflicting reports from the same unit are not uncommon. To muddy the waters still further the group history states that over the target the PFF B-26 Marauder was struck by flak in the right outboard fuel tank three minutes prior to 'bombs away'. Severely damaged, its bombs missed the target, as did the A-26s that dropped their ordnance upon seeing the PFF Marauder's bombs released. The B-26 and a 671st BS A-26 failed to return from the mission, the 416th's combat diary recording, 'Going in on the bomb run, the A-26 flown by Flt Off H J Wilson, with Sgt E F Berkes as his gunner, was seen to nose up and then start downward, still under control. It went in the clouds at 6000 ft and has not been heard from since'. A solitary A-26 also made a crash landing. The 409th BG also lost three Invaders over the target and the 386th BG a B-26.

670th BS pilot Lt Bob Bower was awarded the Air Medal for his actions on the 16th, the pilot giving the following account of the mission upon his return to base;

'Today, Capt Bowman, Lt Chitty and myself really earned our Air Medals. We had a deep penetration, so we had a P-47 escort. We entered Germany north of the Ruhr Valley and turned south to our target. Boy, what a ride that was. I really believe that they had the master sergeants on the guns today. The flak was very, very intense and accurate. Everywhere

Maggie's Drawers **was yet another A-26B assigned to the 416th BG whose serial remains unidentified**

I looked I saw flak. The sky seemed to be filled with the lethal stuff. One curtain of it was so heavy that it seemed that someone had taken a black crayon and coloured out the blue sky. We encountered flak for 15 minutes before we hit the target, as well as over the target itself and for five minutes after we had left the target. Capt Bowman's gunner counted 250 bursts. My gunner called me and said "Wow! You should see the flak back here". For my part, I had all the flak in front of me that I ever wanted to see!

'On our left turn off the target, around Kamen – a heavily-defended town – we caught so much flak I thought the navigator had actually taken us *over* the town. I'm sorry to say that the flak took its toll. Some of the boys saw two B-26s go down and one A-26 exploded. There is no such thing as a glorious part of combat. One of our A-26s had the canopy and bullet-proof glass shot away. Many of the aeroplanes were shot up quite badly. Luckily, only one aeroplane in our flight was hit. Our flight leader, Lt Bob Singletary, really led us in some violent evasive action. It was the most violent formation I ever had to fly. We followed him into very steep turns, dives and climbs. His evasive action was jerky and sudden. Had it not been for such violent evasive flying I am sure we would all have had it.'

On 19 February the group's target was the ordnance depot at Wiesbaden, and as it was anticipated that it would be obscured by bad weather, this was a PFF-led mission. Little flak was encountered and the weather prevented visual observation and photography of the bombing results. All aircraft returned to Laon at the end of the four-hour mission. Bad weather prevented the group from flying again until the 21st, when it flew two missions. The morning target was the communications centre at Geldern. The only written description of the mission comes from the 668th BS history, which reports the results as 'satisfactory'.

For the afternoon mission there were two targets, but for reasons unexplained to the group half of its A-26s, accompanied by half the aircraft of the 410th BG, attacked the Lage-Bielefeld railway bridge. The other target was the communications centre at Geldern, which was attacked for the second time that day by a formation comprising both groups' remaining aircraft. This was the first time that the Ninth Bombardment Division had sent a formation consisting of aircraft from two different groups to the same target. The 669th and 670th BSs represented the 416th BG's contribution.

Over the target the formation encountered accurate flak, and the A-26 flown by Lt R K Johnson of the 669th BS was hit in an engine. Forced to return to base on the remaining powerplant, Johnson managed to retain control of the severely crippled aircraft, but as he approached the runway for an emergency landing it became increasingly difficult to control. He pulled up, thinking that he was going to overshoot the runway, but the bomber lost power as he turned into the dead engine. The A-26 stalled at

The wreckage of the A-26B flown by Lt R K Johnson of the 669th BS, which crashed upon returning from the mission to Geldern on 21 February 1945. The aircraft had had an engine knocked out by flak over the target, and it stalled in just short of the Laon runway, killing a pilot from the 670th BS who was watching the landings. Two of his squadronmates were badly injured, although Johnson and his gunner survived. The wreckage had been moved to this site on the edge of the airfield following its recovery

Lt Johnson's Invader was not the only A-26 written off by the group on 21 February, as this A-26B-20-DL from the 671st BS crashed heavily on landing too. The force of the impact with the ground twisted and broke the nose gear clean off, while the left main gear leg was driven up through its wheel well. Both pilot and gunner survived the crash-landing unscathed

this point and crashed into a wooden shack near to where several pilots from the 670th BS were standing watching the landings. Lts Cooke, Merritt and Sheley were hit, and Cooke died at the scene of the accident. Merritt and Sheley were seriously injured and rushed to hospital, while Johnson was trapped for an hour before the wreckage could be cut away to release him. He had suffered a broken collarbone and facial cuts. The gunner escaped uninjured. It took three days to remove the mangled wreckage from the tent area. It was a miracle that Johnson had been able to retain control of his aircraft for as long as he did.

The remaining 416th and 410th BG crews did not bomb Geldern, as for reasons not stated in the 668th BS history they attacked a secondary target. The results were unobserved and no flak was encountered. The 416th element of the formation returned to Laon after 2 hrs 45 min.

According to the 416th BG history, on the 22nd 'Marauder, Invader and Havoc fleets of the Ninth Bombardment Division swept over Germany's vast railroad and communication systems bombing and strafing bridges and other rail targets in a 200-mile arc running from the Hanover area northeast of the Ruhr to the Saar Valley. Combined with the Eighth Air Force, the RAF and the tactical air forces on the continent, this was one of the most spectacular displays of air power to date. In most cases the aeroplanes bombed from their regular altitudes and then dropped down to the deck to strafe. Almost every section of Germany was hit by one of the air forces during the afternoon and night of operations.

'The 416th did its share of disrupting the German rail system by taking four targets – bridges in the Miltenberg area, sidings and bridges at Höchst, the Münster railway bridge and the Simmern marshalling yard. After bombs away all ships dropped to deck level and strafed at random.'

The group flew two missions on this day, one in the morning and one in the afternoon. The first target to be attacked was the bridge at Münster, the 670th BS history noting that the results from the mission were 'undetermined'. In the afternoon the group made a combined bombing and strafing attack on several targets in Germany. While the 416th had flown strafing missions in the recent past, this was the first time that all the aircraft involved were fitted with the two twin-gun pods under each wing. This brought the total number of guns available in each A-26 to 18 – six in the nose, eight in the pods under each wing and two in each of the gun turrets. Crews were briefed to attack multiple targets and

An armourer from the 668th BS checks over a variety of ordnance prior to loading some of it into the bomb-bay of A-26B-20-DL 41-39274 *Sugar Baby* at Laon

several flights were assigned the same primary target.

Three flights of A-26s from the 416th approached their primary target of two bridges at Miltenberg but found them obscured by haze. They attacked the alternate target – a bridge and siding near Höchst – instead, one flight bombing with excellent results while the second missed the target entirely. The third attacked a bridge at Gochsheim, cutting the tracks at several points. A further flight bombed marshalling yard at Simmern.

The group history stated that 'After completing their bombing attacks the flights peeled off and strafed in the vicinity of the targets, later re-assembling at the rally point. However, a number of the ships returned on their own. Strafing at speeds up to 425 mph, all crews reported shooting up some type of target from horse drawn vehicles to rail stations, buildings, motor convoys and trains. Capt S M Hixon, flying his first mission since 15 December 1944, chalked up the two outstanding strafe jobs of the day. He and his gunner, Sgt K W Schmidt, picked out a motor convoy. In his own words, "We roared down a road and I saw two German trucks standing in the centre. The drivers were running for a ditch, where I saw a number of people taking cover. Both trucks were burning as we pulled away". Sgt Schmidt in the turret also managed to pour some lead into a chain of railroad cars. Capt L J Sutton and his gunner, SSgt D C Gilliam, strafed a long tank train and set it on fire as nose, wing and turret guns poured ammunition the length of the train.'

Following the strafing attack, the group claimed one tank train destroyed and left burning, three heavy motor transports destroyed, one railway station damaged, five locomotives damaged, 15 buildings damaged, one light motor transport damaged and five barges and 15 goods wagons damaged. No flak was encountered, and only sporadic small arms fire challenged the group's aircraft as they roared across the countryside strafing anything and everything they could find. Only two A-26s were hit by small arms fire, but they suffered only light damage.

On 23 February the target was the Golzheim communications centre in Germany, and 39 aircraft from the 416th, led by a PFF Marauder, dropped their bombs through scattered cloud from 13,500 ft. Post-strike photography rated the results as excellent. Neither flak nor fighters were encountered during the mission, and once again all aircraft landed safely back at Laon. The next day's target was the communications centre at Viersen, which was bombed in support of US troops advancing towards Cologne. Taking off in the early afternoon, the group expected the target to be obscured by bad weather. Inaccurate light to heavy flak was encountered, and over the target the group met the anticipated cloud cover – crews bombed in box formation from altitudes of 11,500 ft to 12,500 ft using *Gee*. Heavy flak damaged 11 aircraft over the target but there were no casualties. The cloud cover prevented both visual

43

observation and photography of the bombing results. All aircraft and crews landed safely at Laon.

The weather improved sufficiently for the group to fly two missions on 25 February. In the morning the 416th was again supporting US forces driving on Cologne by attacking the communications centre at Kerpen. Over the target heavy flak claimed the 669th BS A-26 flown by Lt Farley, who had initially led the formation when the aircraft of Lt Col D L Willetts was slowed after take-off with a faulty undercarriage. No parachutes were seen leaving Farley's bomber, which having been hit in the right engine rolled onto its back and then spun out of formation. Several crews subsequently reported seeing the A-26 explode, and a piece of wreckage struck Lt T E Graeber's bomber in the wing leading edge.

Bombing results were mixed, despite good weather over the target. The first box bombed visually and its results were rated as excellent. However, the second box inexplicably chose to bomb by PFF. The results are not mentioned in group or squadron histories. Although the aircraft on the right side of the formation were hit by flak over the target, the damage was light. The A-26 from the first box was the group's only loss of the day.

In the afternoon the group targeted the communications centre at Nörvenich in support of the US Ninth and First Armies, which were advancing through the area. The bombers were accompanied by a 'window'-carrying aircraft to confuse enemy radar and disrupt the flak batteries. The target was obscured by cloud and bombing was accomplished by PFF from an altitude of 13,000 ft. Visual observation and photography of the results was impossible. No flak or fighters were encountered and all aircraft returned safely to Laon, landing at dusk.

On 27 February the weather prevented all flying, but the following day there was an early afternoon take-off for an attack on the ordnance depot at Unna. As it was anticipated that the target would be obscured, this was a PFF and *Gee* mission, with bombing accomplished from 12,500 ft. As usual the weather prevented both visual observation and photography of the bombing results, but it also kept the flak batteries silent and the enemy fighters grounded during the four-hour mission.

The 416th flew its 218th mission on 1 March when it targeted the ordnance depot at Giessen, east of the River Rhine. One of the group's A-26s carried 'window' and there was also a PFF B-26 assigned as it was expected that the target would be obscured by cloud. At this point the histories of the 668th and 670th differ on the mission details. The 668th's states that the group arrived over the target without encountering fighters or flak and found it to be completely obscured. Using PFF and *Gee*, they bombed from 12,000 ft. As usual, weather prevented visual observation and photography of the results. The 670th history states that 'Because of PFF failure, and the fact that they could not locate their fighter escort, the formation turned back and bombed the secondary target of Brunn with the use of their *Gee* equipment. No flak was experienced and no enemy aircraft were encountered. The cloud cover was ten-tenths'.

That the two squadrons' accounts should differ is understandable because the information on which the reports were based comes from different sources. The group returned to Laon without incident and all aircraft landed safely. The following morning the group sent a PFF Marauder and two boxes of A-26s to bomb the motor transport depot at

A-26B-15-DT 43-22385 *BULA* was operated by the 668th BS/416th BG at A55 Melun from late 1944

Iserlohn with 500-lb fragmentation bombs fitted with a new type of airburst fuse that was detonated via radar. No flak or fighters were encountered and bombing was accomplished by PFF from 13,000 ft to 13,500 ft. As the weather prevented visual observation and photography of the target, the results were listed as undetermined.

On 3 March the group was able to celebrate the first anniversary of the start of its combat missions in the ETO. Aircrews marked the occasion with a return to the ordnance depot at Giessen, where cloud cover determined that bombs were released on a signal from the PFF aircraft. As usual the weather prevented visual observation and photography of bombing results, which were reported as undetermined. All crews returned to Laon without having encountered flak or fighters.

The following afternoon the target for the group's 221st mission was the marshalling yard at Lenkerbeck, northwest of Dortmund. The mission had been briefed for the morning but for unrecorded reasons it was delayed. The bombers were led by a PFF Marauder and there was no visual observation or photography. There was no flak or enemy fighters either, and all aircraft returned to Laon and landed safely.

On the 5th 41 aircraft loaded with 500-lb GP bombs took off to attack marshalling yards at Marburg on a PFF-led mission, the results of which were rated as undetermined due to the weather over the target. All aircraft returned safely to Laon without encountering flak or fighters. The target for the afternoon was the marshalling yards at Bingen am Rhein. On a signal from the leading PFF B-26, all 40 A-26 crews released their 500-lb GP bombs from 12,500 ft. The weather over the target precluded visual observation or photography of the results. The following day's target was the marshalling yard at Opladen, and the group was led by a PFF Marauder. There was also a fighter escort. Bombing was from 12,400 ft on the lead B-26's signal, and results were rated as undetermined.

Bad weather caused the next day's mission to be scrubbed, but conditions were better on the 8th and one operation was scheduled. The target was the Wülfrath motor transport depot, housed in a large castle and eight smaller buildings east of Düsseldorf. All crews dropped from 13,500 ft on the signal from the PFF Marauder leading the group. No flak or fighters were encountered and all aircraft returned to Laon. On the 9th the Butzbach marshalling yard was attacked in the morning, followed by the ammunition filling plant at Wulfen – the latter was one of the largest factories manufacturing artillery and anti-aircraft shells in Germany.

The crew composition of the lead A-26C on the Wulfen missions was changed on this date. The usual crew for the lead bombers (group and box lead) consisted of a pilot, gunner and two bombardier/navigators – one to do the navigation while the other dropped the bombs – allowing each to concentrate on just one job. Crowded into the bomber leading the group on 9 March was the CO of the 97th Combat Bombardment Wing, Brig Gen Edward N Backus, who intended to observe the group in action.

At briefing the target was predicted to be completely obscured by bad weather, and this was how it turned out. Bombs were dropped from 12,000 ft to 13,000 ft on the PFF Marauder's signal. The results of the first box were rated as undetermined, but a hole briefly appeared in the cloud over the target, allowing the crews to see the second box's bombs exploding. Several violent explosions of storage buildings were observed and the results were rated as good. The group encountered weak to heavy, yet inaccurate, flak over the target, but no fighters were sighted at any time during the mission. Elsewhere, six of the 11 groups despatched by the Ninth Bombardment Division that morning had seen enemy fighters in what proved to be the Luftwaffe's 'biggest show' against medium bombers since the Battle of the Bulge. 30 Fw 190s attacked A-26s of the 386th BG over Wiesbaden and shot three bombers down.

By this point in the war German military resources were rapidly diminishing. Ground units and aircraft, especially fighters, had to be employed according to priorities. Heavy bombers of the USAAF's Eighth Air Force and RAF Bomber Command had to be stopped at all costs or Germany would have no chance of winning the war. The Luftwaffe duly concentrated on the 'heavies' and their escorting fighters. If any fighters were available they were usually held in reserve unless the medium bombers were attacking their airfields or a target nearby. Otherwise, it was normal for the medium bombers to be unopposed by fighters.

Just one mission was flown on the 10th, with the marshalling yard at Niederscheld being the target. Two aircraft rather than the usual one were carrying 'window' on this occasion. If the group's crews were beginning to regard the description of the weather at briefing as suggesting that they were stuck in a rut they had good reason to believe so – bad weather had seemingly become the rule rather than the exception. The bombers released their loads from 12,800 ft on signal and the results were rated as undetermined. No flak or fighters were encountered during the mission.

The 416th BG flew two missions on 11 March. The morning's target was the airfield at Lippe, northwest of Giessen, and this represented the group's first attack on a Luftwaffe base. It had been reported that aircraft operating from this base were harassing Allied troops crossing the Rhine, so its destruction was given the highest priority. Arriving over the target, crews saw that it was completely obscured by cloud. Bombs were dropped on a signal from the PFF Marauder at 13,000 ft and the results were unobserved by visual observation or photography. All aircraft returned to Laon without encountering flak or enemy fighters.

The afternoon target was the ammunition filling station at Wulfen, which the group had attacked just 48 hours earlier. As was becoming customary, the group was led by a PFF B-26, and one of its aircraft carried 'window' to disrupt enemy radars. On signal from the PFF aircraft the crews released their 500-lb GP bombs from up to 15,000 ft. The weather prevented visual observation and photography of the results, which were rated as undetermined. No enemy fighters or flak were encountered.

Two missions were again flown the next day. The target for the morning PFF mission was the marshalling yard at Lorch, with bombs being released from 15,000 ft and results rated as undetermined. In the afternoon the 416th visited the Posen marshalling yard and bombs were released from 12,500 ft on a signal from the lead PFF aircraft. Due to cloud cover over the target, where there was light flak, the results were again reported as undetermined. All the attackers safely returned to Laon.

There were two missions again on the 13th as pressure increased on the Ninth Bombardment Division to support Allied forces crossing the Rhine. The morning target was another unique one for the group – the Luftwaffe airfield at Rheine. Although the group had already visited

Lippe on 11 March, Rheine was one of the bases operating the pioneering Me 262 jet fighter. Its destruction was given the highest priority as a result. When the 416th crews arrived over the base they found that it was completely obscured by cloud. As was becoming routine, it was briefed and flown as a PFF mission. The aircraft bombed from 9000 ft, with the results unobserved and, accordingly, recorded as undetermined. No enemy fighters were encountered, jet-propelled or otherwise. There was weak to moderate flak at the target, however, and several aircraft in the formation received minor damage but all returned safely to Laon.

The Nieheim marshalling yard was the target for the afternoon, and because of poor weather it too was PFF-led. The target was obscured by cloud cover, but just as the formation arrived there was a small break in the undercast which allowed observation of a portion of the target for a brief moment. But then suddenly, and without warning, the PFF aircraft broke away from the formation and left the target area. This, it was later learned, was because its crew believed the 416th could bomb visually through the hole in the clouds. The PFF crew also stated that they did not inform the formation of their decision to break away because their radio was inoperable. For whatever reason, the formation bombed visually through the hole, which closed up immediately after release. The results were recorded as undetermined due to the cloud cover.

While the crews did not report any flak, at least one A-26 encountered an enemy fighter. A lone Bf 109 attacked it from behind and the Invader gunner promptly fired at it with both turrets but made no damage claims. The formation returned without further incident or excitement to Laon.

On the 14th the group attacked the Nieder-Marsberg railway bridge 60 miles east of Dortmund. The briefed intention of the mission was to disrupt, if not completely halt, traffic using this important double-track crossing over the Ruhr. Almost every mission flown by the group in the last month had been PFF-led due to miserable weather conditions, but on this occasion the crews received a pleasant surprise during the mission briefing – the target was forecast as being clear. And when the crews arrived over the target they found the weather conditions to be almost perfect. They unloaded 100 1000-lb GP bombs, achieving results rated by visual observation as excellent. Target photography duly confirmed that the tracks on both sides of the bridge had indeed been torn up, rendering the line useless for a considerable period of time.

On 15 March the 416th BG, along with five other medium bomber groups, attacked the town of Pirmasens, which was being used as a communications centre. The group history recorded that '45 A-26s were sent out, with six flights hitting the town with incendiaries and one flight dropping frags on two flak positions in the target area. Ratings by flight could not be made as bursts were not visible on the strike photos, but all bombs fell into one large pattern in the centre of town. A large number of fires were started and severe damage was done to buildings in the centre of town. Crews carrying the frag bombs reported excellent results on the flak positions, although due to the type of bomb, no strike photos were available. Although the skies were crystal clear, only a couple of flak bursts were seen and the group did not have any battle damage'.

No missions were flown on the 16th, but there were two the following day. The morning target was the Altenkirchen communications centre, while in the afternoon the A-26s bombed the Bad Homburg marshalling yard. Due to the return of bad weather over the targets, both missions were led by a PFF Marauder equipped with *Gee*. The bombing results were recorded as undetermined.

On the morning of 18 March the group targeted the Worms communications centre. The following account of what proved to be a harrowing mission comes directly from the history of the 670th BS;

'Excellent results were achieved in the attack on the Worms Communication Centre. Intense accurate flak was met. Thirteen of our crews participated in the attack and all returned safely, although the group lost a total of four aircraft. Lt Chitty's aeroplane was hit by flak on the bomb run, and his account of the incident follows;

'"I was flying the No 2 position of the second flight, first box. This was a PFF mission, but as we crossed the bomb line the weather was CAVU (Clear Altitude Vision Unlimited). We reached the IP (Initial Point) flying at 11,500 ft and 200 mph, made a right turn and levelled off for the bomb run. My gunner, Sgt Raccio, called several flak bursts level at 'six o'clock'. At the same time there was a loud explosion and the left engine quit. I advanced the RPM to my good engine and stayed in formation. Ten seconds later another burst in front of me knocked three holes in my windshield and one in the canopy, spraying me with powdered glass. We opened the bomb-bay doors and I made several attempts to feather my left engine, with no results. I left my prop control in full decrease RPM to cut down drag.

'"One minute before bombs away I heard two other explosions, and Sgt Raccio got on the intercom to tell me that there were several small pieces of metal from the top of the bomb-bay laying in his compartment. He had also spotted holes in the tail and wings. Moments later I saw my flight leader's bombs go away, so I pressed the release button. Sgt Raccio called bombs away. I knew I couldn't stay in formation during evasive action, so I peeled out of formation and came back across the bomb line alone.

'"As soon as I was across the bomb line I began checking my instruments and noticed that the fuel pressure on the left engine was down. I advanced RPM and throttle and switched on high boost. The left engine sputtered a few times and caught up, although the fuel pressure was still only ten pounds. The formation was circling at the RP

Groundcrew work on an Invader from the 416th BG at Laon in the early spring of 1945. This is a late production A-26B with the revised 'bubble canopy' which was also known as the 'clamshell' canopy. Delivery of the first A-26s with this revised canopy began in December 1944. Interestingly, this A-26 has had D-Day stripes applied to the underside of its rear fuselage

COLOUR PLATES

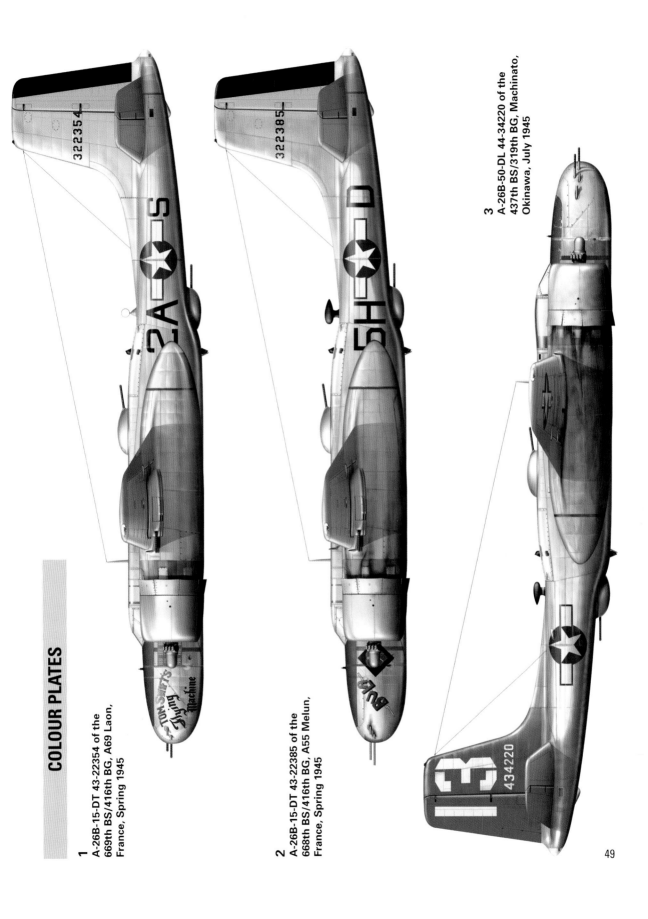

1
A-26B-15-DT 43-22354 of the
669th BS/416th BG, A69 Laon,
France, Spring 1945

2
A-26B-15-DT 43-22385 of the
668th BS/416th BG, A55 Melun,
France, Spring 1945

3
A-26B-50-DL 44-34220 of the
437th BS/319th BG, Machinato,
Okinawa, July 1945

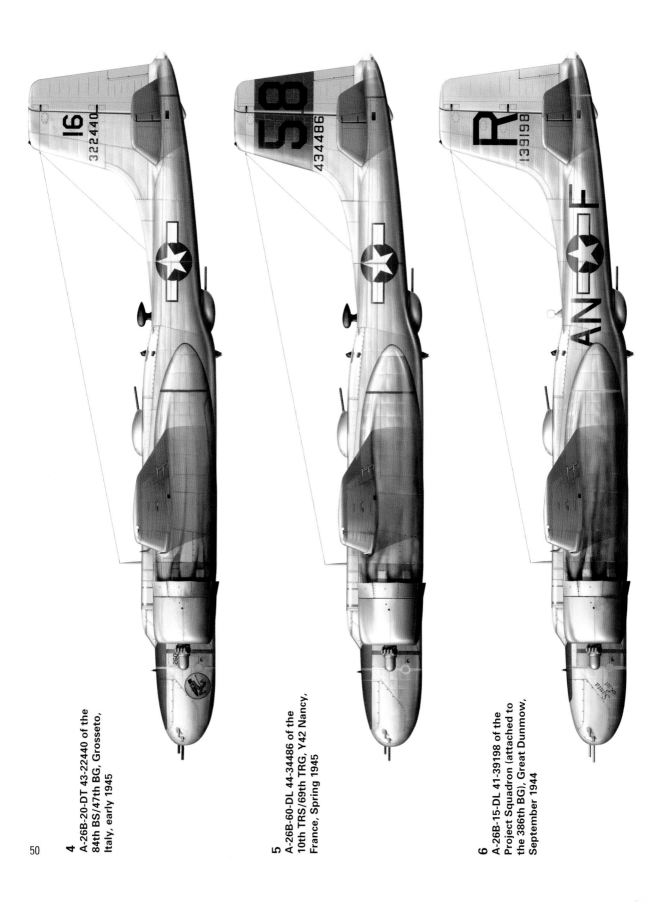

50

4
A-26B-20-DT 43-22440 of the
84th BS/47th BG, Grosseto,
Italy, early 1945

5
A-26B-60-DL 44-34486 of the
10th TRS/69th TRG, Y42 Nancy,
France, Spring 1945

6
A-26B-15-DL 41-39198 of the
Project Squadron (attached to
the 386th BG), Great Dunmow,
September 1944

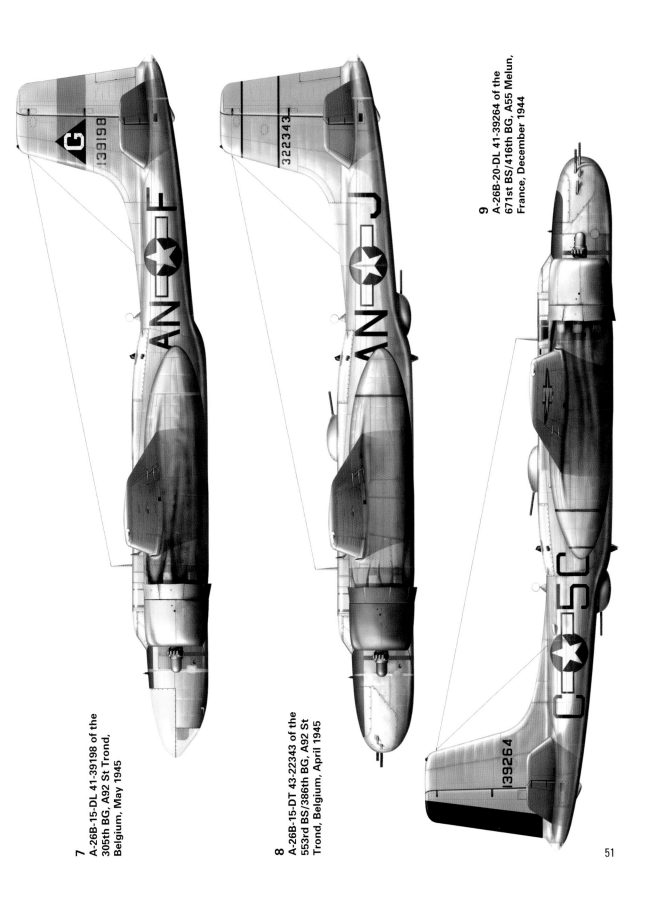

7
A-26B-15-DL 41-39198 of the
305th BG, A92 St Trond,
Belgium, May 1945

8
A-26B-15-DT 43-22343 of the
553rd BS/386th BG, A92 St
Trond, Belgium, April 1945

9
A-26B-20-DL 41-39264 of the
671st BS/416th BG, A55 Melun,
France, December 1944

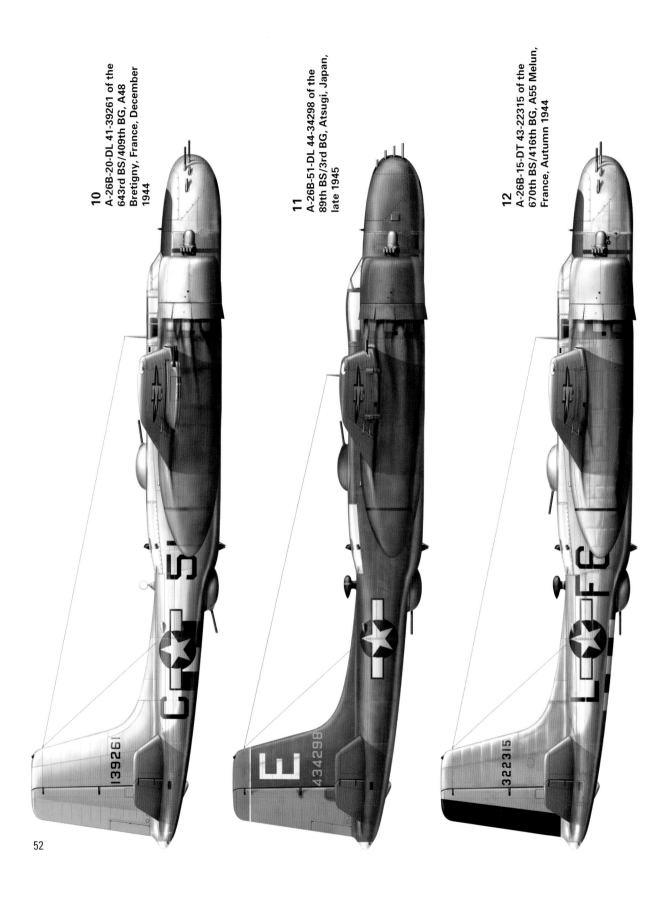

10
A-26B-20-DL 41-39261 of the
643rd BS/409th BG, A48
Bretigny, France, December
1944

11
A-26B-51-DL 44-34298 of the
89th BS/3rd BG, Atsugi, Japan,
late 1945

12
A-26B-15-DT 43-22315 of the
670th BS/416th BG, A55 Melun,
France, Autumn 1944

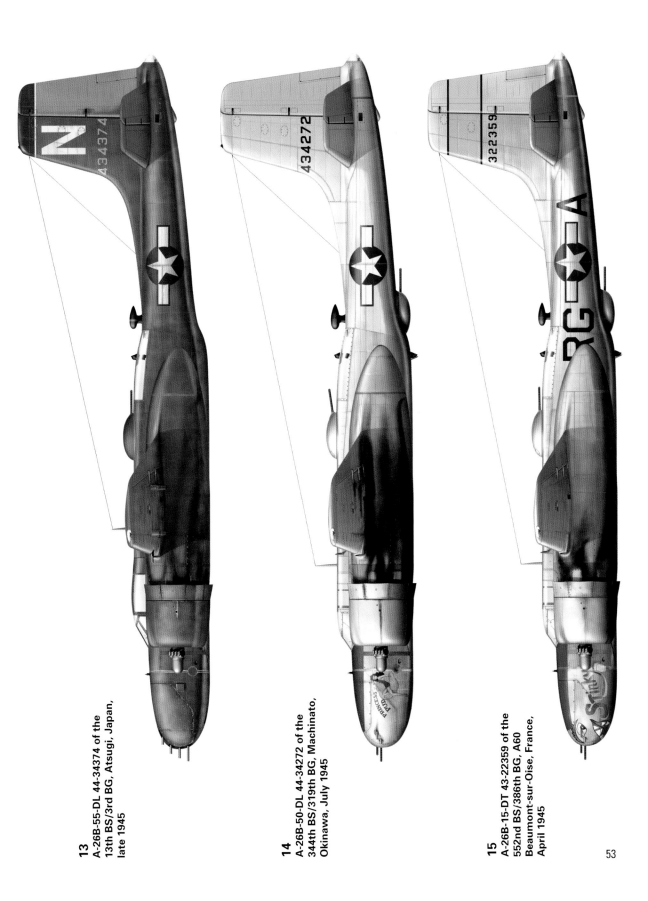

13
A-26B-55-DL 44-34374 of the
13th BS/3rd BG, Atsugi, Japan,
late 1945

14
A-26B-50-DL 44-34272 of the
344th BS/319th BG, Machinato,
Okinawa, July 1945

15
A-26B-15-DT 43-22359 of the
552nd BS/386th BG, A60
Beaumont-sur-Oise, France,
April 1945

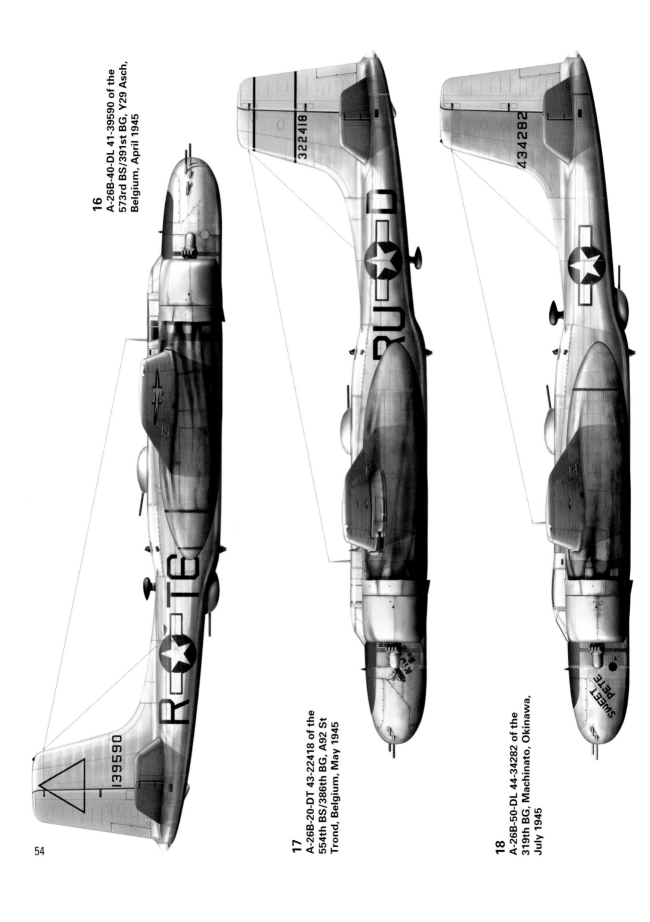

54

16
A-26B-40-DL 41-39590 of the
573rd BS/391st BG, Y29 Asch,
Belgium, April 1945

17
A-26B-20-DT 43-22418 of the
554th BS/386th BG, A92 St
Trond, Belgium, May 1945

18
A-26B-50-DL 44-34282 of the
319th BG, Machinato, Okinawa,
July 1945

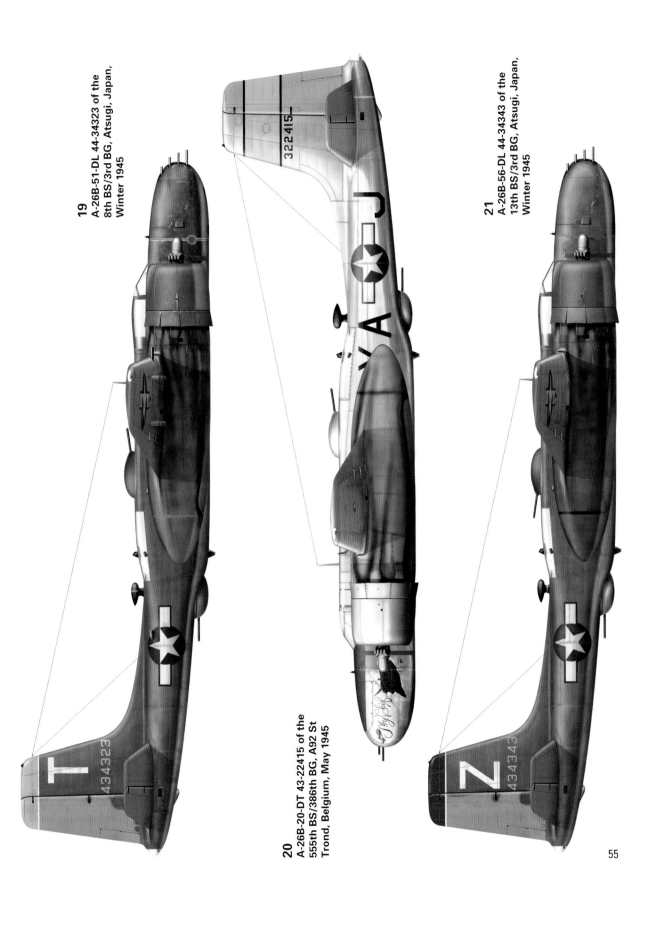

19
A-26B-51-DL 44-34323 of the
8th BS/3rd BG, Atsugi, Japan,
Winter 1945

20
A-26B-20-DT 43-22415 of the
555th BS/386th BG, A92 St
Trond, Belgium, May 1945

21
A-26B-56-DL 44-34343 of the
13th BS/3rd BG, Atsugi, Japan,
Winter 1945

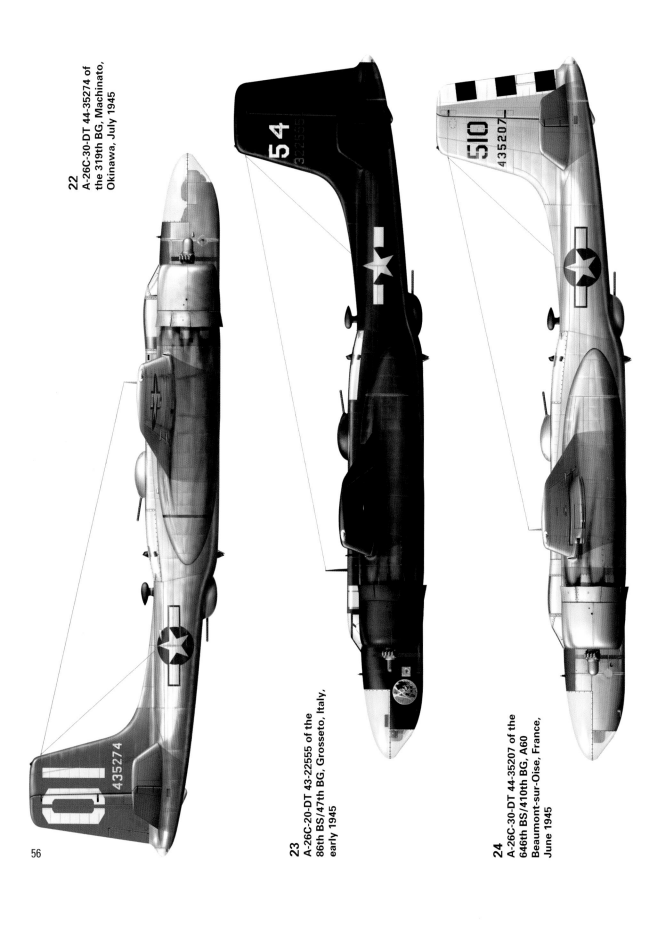

22
A-26C-30-DT 44-35274 of
the 319th BG, Machinato,
Okinawa, July 1945

23
A-26C-20-DT 43-22555 of the
86th BS/47th BG, Grosseto, Italy,
early 1945

24
A-26C-30-DT 44-35207 of the
646th BS/410th BG, A60
Beaumont-sur-Oise, France,
June 1945

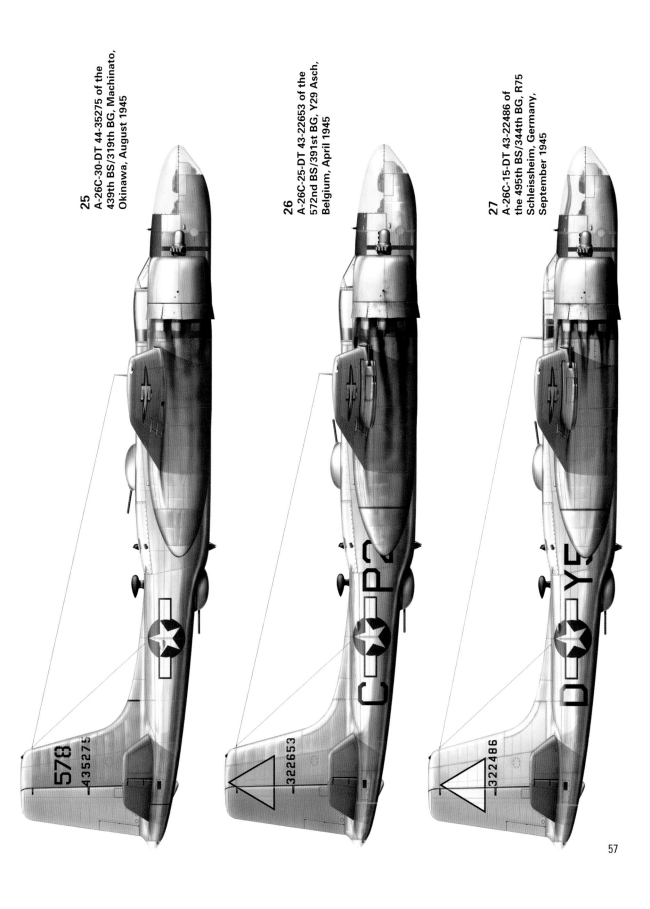

25
A-26C-30-DT 44-35275 of the
439th BS/319th BG, Machinato,
Okinawa, August 1945

26
A-26C-25-DT 43-22653 of the
572nd BS/391st BG, Y29 Asch,
Belgium, April 1945

27
A-26C-15-DT 43-22486 of
the 495th BS/344th BG, R75
Schleissheim, Germany,
September 1945

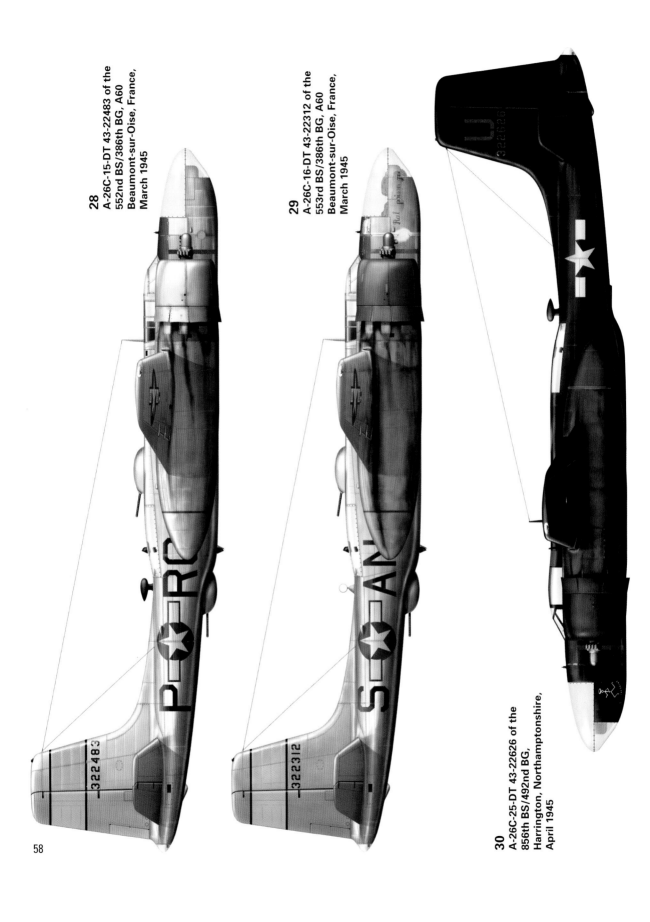

28
A-26C-15-DT 43-22483 of the
552nd BS/386th BG, A60
Beaumont-sur-Oise, France,
March 1945

29
A-26C-16-DT 43-22312 of the
553rd BS/386th BG, A60
Beaumont-sur-Oise, France,
March 1945

30
A-26C-25-DT 43-22626 of the
856th BS/492nd BG,
Harrington, Northamptonshire,
April 1945

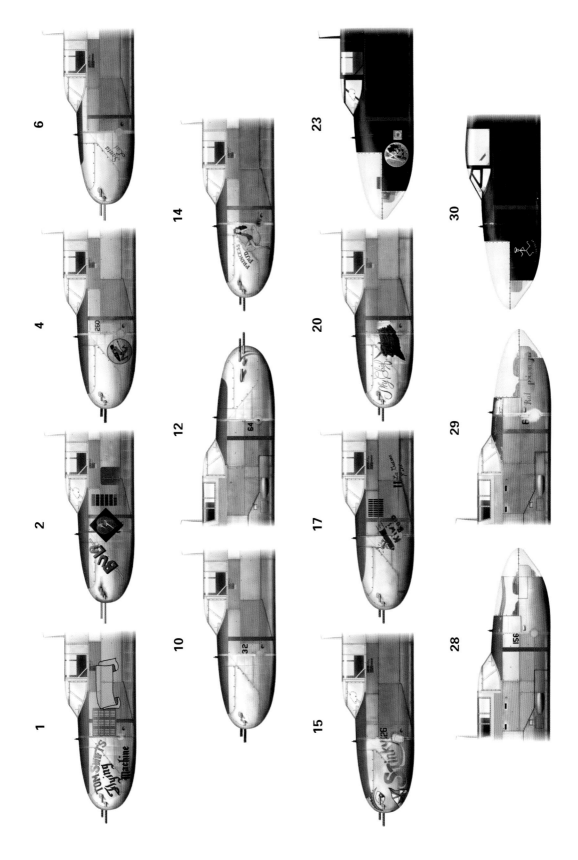

59

1

2

3

4

5

(Rendezvous Point), so I rejoined my flight and we set course to our base. Ten minutes after setting course, Sgt Raccio called that he could see smoke coming into his compartment. I told him to locate the fire and try putting it out. A couple of minutes later he called again and told me that it was apparently gasoline vapour burning out of holes in the top of the bomb-bay tank. He also said the smoke in his compartment was getting thick, so I told him to come up to the pilot's compartment, which he did. I tried to contact my leader but could not do so. Then I tried all emergency channels without success. Sgt Raccio then used the fire extinguisher in the pilot's compartment on the fire but could do no more than slow it down temporarily.

'"As the bomb-bay tank was full of gas, I didn't think there was too much danger of an explosion from the vapour, so I decided to stay with the flight back to our base or until I saw a field. After about 30 minutes I saw our field, so I peeled off and called in for an emergency landing. I could hear 'Boat Deck' control very faintly but could not understand them. Once I was sure of making the runway I cut all switches and cut my gas off. As soon as the wheels touched, Sgt Raccio opened the hatch. I let the aeroplane roll on at the end of the runway so as to be clear of other A-26s, after which we climbed out. The fire department was at the aeroplane as soon as it stopped rolling. I believe the bomb-bay tank being full of gasoline is all that prevented an explosion, as the vapour escaping from the flak holes in the top of the tank was burning. The gas vapour apparently caught fire from electrical wiring inside the bomb-bay that had been severed by pieces of flak.'"

The 671st BS suffered its worst single mission losses with the A-26 during this mission, as detailed in its combat history;

'The 416th BG encountered another "Bloody Sunday" on 18 March with the loss of four ships and crews over the target area. The A-26s were despatched in the morning with a PFF lead, but the skies were clear over the target and bombing was done visually as the flak gunners threw up everything but the kitchen sink. The 671st BS suffered on the morning mission when Lt W R Jokinen and his gunner, SSgt E J Creeden, were shot down over the target. No 'chutes were seen and the ship was followed to the ground. This was Lt Jokinen's 17th mission and Creeden's 10th. Capt Cornell, Lt Vars and Lt Kinney and their crews were also lost.'

Jokinen and Creeden were duly captured after performing a textbook belly landing.

In the afternoon the 416th shifted its attention to the Cologne sector, where the clouds were thick and heavy and the flak nil. The A-26s, led by a PFF aircraft, attacked the Kreuztal marshalling yard, located at a junction of two main lines leading north from the Giessen-Cologne line. Traffic at this centre had increased greatly in recent weeks. The results of the raid were unobserved.

A-26B *Miss Mildred* was flown by 670th BS pilot Lt Edward Bishop, who later retired from the USAF with the rank of colonel. His son, G Knox Bishop, would also later serve as a USAF pilot and retire as a colonel too

There were three missions for the group the next day. Two were flown simultaneously and with separate boxes of 21 and 24 aircraft, the first being an attack on the Lage railway bridge which was bombed by a box from the 416th led by Maj C H Ferris, CO of the 670th BS. The formation encountered moderate but accurate flak for five minutes after reaching the bomb line. There was an escort of P-38 fighters, but they found no German aircraft. The formation bombed visually, with results rated as superior. Meanwhile, a further box of 416th bombers attacked the road junction at Nassau. No flak or fighters were encountered, and bombing results were recorded as excellent.

In the afternoon the target was the Schwelm marshalling yard, where weak and inaccurate flak was encountered and no aircraft were damaged. Bombing was accomplished visually, and the results were reported as excellent. The bombers, led by a box of A-26s from the 409th BG, were escorted by P-38s and P-47s, but no enemy aircraft were encountered.

The target assigned to the group on the 20th was the Giesecke marshalling yard, but it could not be located due to severe weather blanketing the target area. The group therefore bombed the secondary target of Westerberg instead, and this was accomplished visually and with no opposition from flak or fighters at any time. The results were rated as excellent. All aircraft returned to Laon.

The Goesfeld communications centre in Holland was attacked by the group on the morning of 21 March, with bombing being accomplished visually and results rated as superior. No flak or fighters were encountered and all aircraft returned to base without incident. The entry in the 670th history for the second mission of the day read as follows;

'That afternoon another mission took off and attacked Vreden road junction and communication centre with excellent results. Fourteen of our crews took part.

'Capt Rooney was leading his flight homeward into the setting sun at about 12,000 ft when another flight leader, who was also flying into the sun, collided with him. Apparently Capt R J Rooney tried to get his aeroplane under control in an attempt to save his crew, but it went into a spin and crashed near Peers, Belgium. All personnel in both A-26s were killed instantly when their aircraft crashed into the ground, with the exception of 1Lt Robert L Kirk, Capt Rooney's bombardier/navigator, who successfully parachuted to the ground. Capt Chester C Slaughter of the 29th Infantry Division, who was riding as an observer with Capt Rooney, and Sgt Robert J Kamischke, the gunner, were killed. Three officers and one enlisted man in the other aeroplane were also killed. This was Capt Rooney's 65th mission, and constituted his tour of duty.'

671st BS aircraft await their next mission at Laon in early 1945. As this photograph clearly reveals, conditions at the airfield were austere to say the least

On 22 March the group attacked the Borken communications centre, a single bomber crash-landing at Venlo after dropping its ordnance. The 416th's combat history noted that 'Lt D A Fero had a harrowing experience on this mission. He received hits in the left engine coming in to the target. At the same time his right engine began to leak oil. He salvoed his bombs and headed for friendly territory. It was all he could do to keep the A-26 in the air until he finally spotted the airfield at Venlo. After dropping his bombs, his bomb-bay doors would not close so he had to pump them up by hand. He racked it back and dropped the aeroplane in on an open field just beyond the airstrip. Making a brilliant crash-landing, neither he nor his gunner, SSgt A A Rojas, were injured'.

Eight flights participated in the morning mission, bombing with superior results. The group returned to Borken in the afternoon and dropped incendiaries via *Gee* because the target was obscured by smoke.

The 23rd saw Ninth Bombardment Division units deliver both morning and afternoon attacks on enemy defences between Münster and the Rhine, with key towns in the German chain of communications in this area bearing the brunt of the strikes. This time it was the turn of Dinslaken to be bombed, as the 670th BS history recalled;

'In the morning, superior results were achieved against a munitions factory with 1000-lb bombs, and again in the afternoon another superior was scored against buildings and roads using 500-lb incendiary bombs. A total of 17 of our crews took part in these two missions. During the morning mission Lt Russell G Ford was shot down and landed within our lines. His interesting account is as follows;

'"The boxes proceeded to the target on time and peeled off at the proper interval from the IP. No flak was experienced on the run, although we were in enemy territory and only two-and-a-half minutes from the target. However, as we closed the bomb-bay doors, preparing for a second run, one burst exploded directly beneath and to the rear of my nacelle. The left fuel pressure immediately dropped off to zero. I tried all gas combinations but with no success, so I feathered the left propeller. My airspeed had fallen to 150 mph and I was losing altitude, which caused me to re-check my fuel pressure.

'"By the time I had rolled out on a reciprocal heading of 223 degrees (our emergency heading) my right fuel pressure was fluctuating, and as I completed my first call to 'Parade', it too dropped to zero. In an effort to keep at least one engine running, I pushed the blowers back into low and tried to start the left engine once more. When nothing happened I pulled the controls back into high blower and made one more attempt.

'"As soon as I had taken up the emergency heading I had not only called 'Parade', (since C channel was jammed) but also notified my gunner, Sgt Tharp, to prepare to bail out. We had dropped to 9000 ft indicated in the turn, and it was then that I checked the time in order to ascertain when I would cross the River Rhine, for we could not see the bomb line due to the smoke blowing from Germany. The time allowed was three-and-a-half minutes. I was descending at a rate of 2000 ft per minute, which I figured would bring me over the bomb line at an altitude of 3500 ft indicated.

'"At 6800 ft, the gunner tried to salvo the bombs without success. Again, I called 'Parade' for a fix, and once more was told to fly a heading of 180 degrees and call in three minutes. Fortunately, I ignored this heading and continued on 223 degrees. Then I hit my own salvo switch. Nothing happened, so I opened the doors in the normal manner and tried to punch the bombs out – this time the arming switch was in neutral.

'"By that time we were at about 3500 ft indicated and my rate of descent had decreased to 1600 ft per minute. The gunner tried unsuccessfully to get the bombs out with the doors open. As a last resort he had to jettison his escape hatch, and at 3800 ft I ordered him out. His acknowledgement was the last words I heard from him. At 3300 ft I felt something hit the tail – whether it was Tharp I could not say. After that I re-hooked my flak suit and harness, since I realised that I had little chance of getting out. I could not reach my flak helmet, however. Afterwards, I made certain all bombing switches were off, and at 2000 ft indicated I started calling off altitude to the gunner in case he was still with me.

'"A town was on my left, with two fields west of it – a road with telephone lines paralleling it separating them. About 200 ft above the ground I dumped full flaps and cut all my switches. I made my turn into the field still maintaining 150 mph with the props feathered. The flare out showed no signs of a stall, and even when my airspeed dropped off to 130 mph I still had control of the aircraft. I was forced to alter my plan to land in the first field when I saw a team of horses in line with me. The aircraft still handled smoothly, allowing me to bank to the left and pass under the telephone lines. I misjudged slightly though and cut one of the wires. Unfortunately, a ditch in the middle of the second field caused me to push the aeroplane into the ground early in order to escape stalling out in the ditch. The 1000 'pounders' stayed in the bomb-bay!"

'Lt Ford suffered a nine-inch laceration of the scalp when the A-26 crashed. Sgt Tharp is reported as being missing in action.'

The 416th made it eight missions in 48 hours on 24 March when it flew two more operations. The first of these was against anti-aircraft gun emplacements near Bocholt, and crews encountered flak that they described as being 'intense but inaccurate'. Bombing was accomplished visually with results rated as excellent. As the group returned to base the crews noticed that 'the sky was filled with C-47s towing gliders, which were heading east to participate in the mass offensive. That afternoon our aeroplanes went out again to attack the Colbe railway bridge'. Having performed a maximum effort mission in the morning, the 416th despatched just four flights in the afternoon, and their efforts were graded as excellent, superior and good. Subsequent reconnaissance flights over the target revealed that the bridge had been completely destroyed.

The following day the group sent 48 aircraft to attack the Altenkirchen communications centre. Once over the target the A-26s endured a heavy flak barrage that saw 22 bombers suffer varying degrees of damage. The Invader flown by Lt Barausky was hit the hardest, with a large part of the nacelle being shot away from the right engine. The pilot feathered the propeller and pulled out of the bomb run, with oil and fuel pouring from his aircraft. The flak hit had bent a portion of the nacelle upwards, causing much drag that hampered the single engine performance of his A-26. Barausky headed for the airfield at Trier to make a forced landing, and just before touching down he cut the left engine and feathered the propeller. The aircraft was irreparably damaged in the dead stick landing but Barausky, his bombardier/navigator and gunner were uninjured.

The target for the afternoon mission was the critically important Fulda marshalling yard, which was a key point for the transfer of supplies and equipment to German troops facing Gen George Patton's forces. Bombing was accomplished visually, with violent explosions of the fuel and ammunition cars observed by the aircrews involved. The results were rated as excellent to superior. No flak was reported, and while enemy fighters were seen in the area, none engaged the 416th BG crews.

On 26 March the group attacked Gemünden marshalling yard, which although some distance from Laon, was just a few miles ahead of Patton's rapidly advancing forces. Bombing was performed visually and the results were rated as excellent. No encounters with flak or fighters were reported.

After chalking up 37 missions in 26 days, the 416th BG was stood down for 24 hours on the 27th when poor weather set in. Conditions had improved sufficiently the following day to allow the group to target the oil storage depot at Erbach. Bombing with the aid of a PFF aircraft via *Gee* and ETA, results were unobserved due to cloud over the target. No flak or fighters were reported, and all aircraft returned to Laon and landed safely.

On the 30th it was the turn of the Hann Munden ordnance depot and barracks area to receive a visit from the group. Again, bad weather prevented visual observation and photography of the bombing, and five aircraft were damaged by flak. The group rounded out its most active month of operations by chalking up missions 41 and 42 on 31 March. The first target was a storage depot in Würzburg that was on the main railway line between Frankfurt and Nuremberg. Crews reported good to excellent results on visual observation, their 500-lb incendiary clusters starting large fires in the block of warehouse buildings.

The afternoon mission on the 31st was flown against Marienburg, across the Main River from Würzburg. According to the group's official history, 'To further deplete the enemy's supplies, the 416th and five other Ninth Bombardment Division groups struck at a storage area in Marienburg. The vast storage area comprised 21 warehouse type and 20 smaller buildings, a permanent barracks area and a large motor park. American tanks and infantry were reported meeting resistance in this area, and crews were told that if the enemy was to counter-attack it probably would be from that point. Box 1 obtained excellent results via the PFF lead, but the pathfinder aircraft of the second box dropped late. There were no losses, casualties or battle damage'. Bad weather over both targets prevented visual observation and photography of the bombing. The results for both missions were rated as undetermined.

A-26s of the 671st BS taxi out to the runway at Laon on the morning of 31 March 1945. Note that the entire left nacelle of A-26B '5C-W' has inexplicably been painted white. The unit attacked storage areas at Würzburg and nearby Marienburg on this date

An anonymous groundcrewman from the 668th BS checks the port wing fuel tank of an A-26. The aircraft visible over his shoulder is *Sugar Baby*

The 670th BS's statistics for the month of March were typical for all four squadrons assigned to the 416th BG, and they reveal just how fully occupied the group had been. The squadron had flown 41 missions and dropped more than 1,300,000 lbs of high explosive, incendiary and fragmentation bombs. According to the squadron history, 'this amount was about equivalent to two-thirds of the total poundage dropped by the 670th in the eight months it employed the A-20 in tactical operations. At times, because of the scarcity of bombs and the great number dropped, it was necessary for squadron ordnance personnel to travel to other bases in order to get enough for the next morning's mission'.

The Ninth Bombardment Division issued this press release detailing the exploits of its medium and light bomb groups in March 1945;

'Commended by Lt Gen Omar N Bradley for its sustained offensive, the Ninth Bombardment Division turned out a record month of operations during which its medium and light bombers flew 15,000 sorties and dropped 24,000 tons of bombs. The March figures set an all time high for Maj Gen Samuel E Anderson's bomber forces, eclipsing the previous record of 10,538 sorties and 15,226 tons established in June 1944. Operational 28 days, including 19 straight days from 8 March through to 26 March, the division's B-26s, A-20s and A-26s ranged over a 250-mile front from Münster Bay south to the Main Scarplands to disrupt road and rail communications and deny the enemy facilities for moving reinforcement equipment and supplies to meet Allied offensives.

'Two-thirds of the division's record assault was directed against communications centres, marshalling yards and bridges on routes feeding battle areas with supplies and reinforcements. Sweeping advances by ground forces over the entire western front testify to the bombers success in blocking German attempts to strengthen defence lines. Successfully completed campaigns to isolate battle areas, including the industrial Ruhr and Remagen bridgehead, resulted in widespread destruction of German transportation facilities. Nine major railway bridges on main lines were destroyed or left unserviceable, four railway overpasses damaged and at least 33 marshalling yards severely damaged. Bomber attacks cut all lines in 20 rail yards and left only one line open in eight others. A total of 584 rail cuts were made. Rail facilities destroyed or damaged included 1769 cars, nine roundhouses, 12 locomotives and 26 workshops.

'Sharing top priority with rail targets in the bombers' March offensive were 81 communications centres – equally important to the German defence in the west. Attacking the towns with 8000 tons of incendiaries and high explosives, the medium and light bombers blocked roads with craters and debris, cut rail lines and levelled warehouses, factories and buildings that would offer protection for house-to-house fighting.

'Destroyed or damaged in the bombers' assault on communications centres were 7851 buildings, 79 factories and 99 warehouses. Main and secondary roads running through the towns were cut in 887 places, two highway overpasses destroyed and six highway bridges damaged.

'A four-day offensive against gun positions, roads and rail lines in and around 21 towns in the area north of the Ruhr where the 21st Army Group is now expanding its Rhine River bridgehead highlighted the bombers' attacks on communication centres. While the main weight of their attacks were aimed at road and rail facilities, the bombers backed up their assault to immobilise the German army by striking at seven fuel and ammunition dumps and ten ordnance and motor vehicles repair depots.

'Twenty-three bombers were lost to flak and enemy fighters during the month against claims of nine enemy fighters destroyed, three probably destroyed and five damaged.'

April ushered in more bad weather, with the 416th grounded at Laon for the first two days of the month. Conditions improved sufficiently by the 3rd to allow the group to fly its 260th combat mission. The target was the Hameln marshalling yard and the mission was a PFF-led one. Bad weather over the target forced the group to bomb from 16,000 ft and prevented visual observation and photography of the target. However, crews of the 669th BS reported that a brief break in the clouds had allowed them to view the bombing, which they reported as good.

The next day's target was a barracks at Crailsheim, as well as the troops based there. Due to the bad weather, this was another PFF-led mission, the crews involved releasing 232 500-lb incendiary bombs on the pathfinder Marauder's signal. Again, the weather prevented visual observation and photography of the bombing. While the results were rated officially as undetermined, all crews felt that they should at least have been good because the PFF equipment functioned perfectly.

Bad weather kept the group from flying further combat missions until 8 April, although it was good enough to permit local training flights to be made. This allowed pilots and crews to build up valuable flight time and to practise formation flying and other procedures. They made up for lost time on the 8th by flying two missions during the course of the day. The Munich-Bernsdorf rail sidings and oil storage tanks were attacked in the morning by seven flights that dropped 150 GP bombs. The 416th was one of four bomb groups to strike the target at 20-minute intervals from 0900 hrs, and smoke could be seen rising from the storage tanks from a distance of 70 miles away. Bombing was accomplished visually, and the crews reported observing violent explosions in the target area. The target of the afternoon mission was the town of Sondershausen and the built-up areas around it. The results achieved by the six flights were rated as excellent, despite the target being covered in haze and smoke.

The group flew two missions the following day, with the Amberg-Kümmersbruck ordnance depot being attacked in the morning. Despite poor weather, the group was able to bomb visually, with results being rated as excellent. In the afternoon the 60 sidings within the Saalfeld marshalling yard were attacked visually, with results rated as excellent.

There were two missions on the 10th as well, and for the first time both targets were located in Czechoslovakia. The morning mission was to the Eger railway viaduct, which was 1344 ft in length. Weather conditions were ideal and the target was bombed visually with superior results – a span was destroyed and numerous buildings in the immediate area hit. In the afternoon 22 A-26s from the 416th BG joined forces with 13 Invaders from the 409th BG to bomb the Stassfurt-Leopoldshell oil storage depot. The attack was directed against storage and loading facilities, including pipelines and underground tanks, and crews reported that the installation was rocked by explosions and blanketed in oily smoke – the latter rose as high as 11,000 ft. Bombing results were rated as excellent overall.

On the 11th the morning target was the Bernburg marshalling yard, which was bombed visually with excellent results. In the afternoon the Zwickau marshalling yard was bombed visually with results again judged as excellent to superior.

The next day, however, rain and cloud over the Kempton ordnance depot prevented bombing, and the 416th formation returned with bombs still on board – the same fate befell seven other groups sent to bomb targets that morning. A bomb broke loose in the bomb-bay of the A-26 flown by Maj Ferris, who was forced to line the aircraft up on a bombing range, open the doors and release his ordnance, thus preventing any mishap caused by the loose weapon. In the afternoon group personnel, together with every other American, were stunned to learn of the death of President Franklin D Roosevelt. Hof railway bridge was attacked by four flights of aircraft during the afternoon, with ordnance being dropped from 5500 ft. Although the weather was poor en route to the target, it cleared sufficiently enough to allow the A-26 crews to render the bridge unserviceable.

More poor weather saw missions scrubbed on 13 and 14 April, but on the morning of the 15th the Ulm marshalling yard was attacked with incendiary bombs in a PFF-led strike. Results of the mission were unobserved. The following day the Invaders hit two marshalling yards southwest of Berlin. Zerbst was the first to be attacked, with incendiaries being dropped on buildings, tracks and rail cars. A fire was started in the centre of the yard, and this was seen to rapidly spread. Flak was encountered on the bomb run too, but no aircraft were damaged. Crews bombed visually and their results were rated as excellent. That afternoon the 416th attacked Wittenburg marshalling yards with undetermined results due to cloud cover. Two aircraft received flak damage.

On the morning of 17 April the group visually bombed the defended town of Magdeburg, which stood in the way of the US Ninth Army's advance across the Elbe River. It was bombed for nearly four hours by 11 bomb groups, the USAAF having been given the order to level the town after US forces had met the heaviest organised resistance in weeks. The Tübingen ordnance depot was attacked in the afternoon, this site supposedly having been stockpiled with stores in preparation for the Nazi regime's proposed final stand in the Bavarian hills. Visual reports from both missions stated that the bombing was highly accurate.

Following a 24-hour break in operations, Ulm marshalling yard was bombed visually with excellent to superior results during the afternoon of 19 April. Enemy fighters were reported in the target area and one approached the formation while it was circling the rally point. A gunner opened fire on the fighter, which immediately broke away and departed without firing at the bombers. The morning raid on the Deggendorf oil storage depot had had to be postponed, however, due to poor weather.

These A-26Bs from the 671st BS clipped wingtips while moving along the taxiway at Laon in poor weather conditions on 2 April 1945

This target was bombed with excellent results on the morning of 20 April, crews seeing smoke from blazing oil fires rising to almost 9000 ft. In the afternoon the group attacked the Annaburg storage depot, again with devastating results. Bombing was performed visually on both occasions.

On the 21st the 416th raided the Attnang-Puchheim marshalling yard in Austria, thus marking the first time a Ninth Bombardment Division unit had attacked a target in that country. Bombing was performed visually from 8000 ft due to cloud, and the results achieved by the seven flights involved were rated as excellent to superior. As the aircraft departed the target area they passed over the Luftwaffe airfield at Erding and encountered light flak, damaging the A-26 flown by Lt Hackley.

No missions were flown for the next 48 hours, but on the 24th the 416th tried to use A-26 pathfinders for the very first time. The target for the day was the Luftwaffe airfield at Landau, and the group was to be guided by PFF (now designated SHORAN – Short Range Air Navigation) Invaders from the 409th BG. However, equipment failure and effective jamming of the *Gee* frequency by the enemy forced the mission to be scrubbed, as the aircraft could not bomb visually.

The target on the 25th was the Freilassing ordnance depot, which was bombed visually. Six flights attacked the target, which was just 20 miles from the Führer's Bavarian headquarters at the Berchtesgarden. The results were rated as superior. Plattling airfield was bombed visually the following day, with results rated as excellent to superior.

Bad weather then prevented any operational flying until 1 May, when the attack on the Stod ammunition depot in Czechoslovakia allowed the group to chalk up mission No 284. Bad weather conditions prevented the group from bombing the target, however, and all 37 aircraft returned home with their bombs. No missions were flown the following day, but on the 3rd the group returned to the Stod plant, and this time all 36 Invaders were able to bomb thanks to the assistance of SHORAN A-26s. Dropping their ordnance from 13,700 ft, crews were unable to determine the accuracy of the attack due to the weather.

The Stod attack proved to be the last combat mission undertaken by the 416th BG, as no sorties were flown on 4, 5 and 6 May. On the latter date group personnel heard the radio announcement that the Germans had surrendered. The war in Europe was over.

A-26C-20-DT 43-22498, nicknamed *Doris Lee*, served with the 416th BG as a lead ship in the final weeks of the war in Europe

MORE UNITS CONVERT

The 416th BG may have been the first of the USAAF's bomb groups to see action in the ETO with the A-26, but it was by no means the only one. Four others would be operational with the attack bomber by VE Day, namely the 409th, 410th, 386th and 391st.

409th BG

The 409th BG became the next Ninth Air Force bomb group to convert to the A-26 following the successful transition of the 416th. Another A-20 unit, it commenced conversion in early December 1944. By then the group had been flying from the A48 Bretigny, a few miles west of Melun, for two-and-a-half months. Having seen action with the A-26 in the Battle of the Bulge, the 409th played a major role in the Ninth Bombardment Division's tactical bombing campaign against targets in western Germany.

For example, on 23 January the 409th joined the 416th and the A-20-equipped 410th BG in the USAAF's first low-level bomber mission in the ETO since the Ijmuiden raid of May 1943. The 409th sent six of its A-26s to bomb and strafe targets of opportunity, but because of adverse weather only one Invader from the 409th was able to identify and attack a target – Lt Arden D Connick of the 643rd BS bombed a concentration of German vehicles near Arzfeld. After dropping his ordnance, Connick strafed a machine gun nest and troops in a nearby village. His aircraft was struck by ground fire, which damaged the rudder. Despite this, he then strafed another gun emplacement, as well as a half-track and two trucks.

As he pulled up from his run, Connick saw that his left engine had been hit and was trailing smoke, while fuel was leaking from the main tank. Disregarding the damage, he began another attack on the same gun emplacement, destroying it and hitting a number of the soldiers manning the weapon. His aircraft was again hit by ground fire, this time in the right engine and the flaps. Even though both engines had been damaged and were on fire, Connick continued his attacks. He strafed three more trucks before it became imperative for him to land before the battle damage took the decision out of his hands. He finally found a clearing large enough to allow a safe crash-landing, but the ground was not level. With a damaged rudder, no flaps and both engines on fire, he managed to put his A-26 down on the side of a hill. Needless to say the aircraft was written off. The fact that he was able to carry out attacks after his Invader had sustained severe damage offered ample testimony to the rugged construction of the A-26.

On 15 February the group moved to its new base, A70 Laon/Couvron, again in France. The next day the 409th sent 29 A-26s, led by eight

A-20s and following a PFF B-26, to attack the ordnance depot at Unna. A-26s from the 416th BG and B-26s from the 386th BG also participated in the mission. Three Invaders from the 409th were shot down by flak, which also downed a 386th Marauder.

As mentioned in the previous chapter, the 409th was the first group in the ETO to employ the A-26 pathfinder operationally when a handful of modified aircraft led Invaders from the 416th BG in a raid on the Luftwaffe airfield at Landau on 24 April. Designated SHORAN Invaders, and built to replace PFF B-26s, the aircraft proved unable to locate the target on this occasion due to a combination of equipment failure and effective jamming of the *Gee* frequency by the enemy.

Like most other medium bomber groups in-theatre, the 409th BG continued to attack targets through to 3 May, with its last mission also being flown against the Stod ammunition depot in Czechoslovakia.

Having lost a substantial portion of its left wing to a direct flak hit during its bomb run, an unidentified A-26B from the 642nd BS/409th BG plummets earthwards

This 386th BG A-26B was forced to make an emergency belly landing at Melun (then home of the 416th BG) on 25 January 1945 after it suffered flak damage. The bent propeller blades indicate that both engines were still running when the aircraft touched down

410th BG

The third A-20-equipped unit in the ETO to switch to the A-26, the 410th BG had moved from Gosfield, in Essex, to A58 Coulommiers, in France, on 18 September 1944. However, unlike the 416th and 409th BGs, it did not immediately replace all of its Havocs with Invaders. The 410th was selected for a new type of mission both for the unit as well as for the USAAF. Four A-26Bs were assigned to the group, which then exchanged its entire complement of gun-nose A-20G/Hs for a similar number of glazed-nose A-20J/Ks. It also received eight B-26s from Marauder groups in the Ninth Bombardment Division.

Once equipped, the 410th was intended to engage in night ground attack and support missions using all three aircraft types, the quartet of Invaders being painted black overall to help conceal them from enemy flak gunners. A Royal Canadian Air Force pilot experienced in night operations was also attached to the group to instruct crews in nocturnal

operations. Eglin Field, Florida, was the USAAF proving ground where new tactics and equipment were evaluated, and also where tactics and procedures for night operations were developed. An instructor pilot from here was attached to the 410th to advise it on the procedures developed there.

The intention was for missions to be flown in the following way. A PFF B-26 would arrive over the target and illuminate it with flares. Two A-26s would then approach the target, one of which was designated the 'master bomber' to direct the activities of the other aircraft in the target area. The other A-26 was designated as 'marker bomber', and it would drop a coloured marker to indicate the target to the following A-20s. Each marker bomb would emit a red, yellow or green trail, which would burn for four minutes. After the marker bomber had dropped his marker the master bomber would direct the A-20s, one at a time, over the target. The A-20 bombardier would release his bombs using the smoke from the marker as his aiming point. The PFF B-26 and the marker bomber would keep the target illuminated until each of the A-20s had dropped their bombs.

Following two practice missions during daylight, the 410th flew the first night mission in late January 1945. After several operations it was determined that the nightfighter units were better suited to such missions, however. On the third operation, a German nightfighter attempted to attack the A-26s, but it was warded off by one of the turret gunners. Following its brief flirtation with night bombing, the 410th BG resumed daylight operations with the A-20, moving to A68 Juvincourt on 14 February. In the event the group did not fully convert to the A-26 until just a few days before the German surrender in early May 1945.

386th BG

The 386th BG was originally assigned to the Eighth Air Force and based at Boxted, in Suffolk, before moving to Great Dunmow, in Essex, in September 1943. When the Ninth Air Force was activated in England on 16 October 1943, the 386th BG was transferred to it, although the unit and the other three medium bomb groups in the

A-26B-15-DL Invader 41-29194 *MISCHIEVOUS MICCS* suffered a nose gear failure on landing at Coulommiers in late 1944. Note the olive drab A-20s parked behind the aircraft

This A-26B-45-DL of the 646th BS/ 410th BG was photographed following its return to the USA in late 1945. The bomber has had all of its armament removed

BEAUTIFUL KATEY of the 386th BG has its port engine serviced on the ramp at Bretigny. It is equipped with dual underwing gun pods

Adorned with a smile, *Stinky* was a colourful A-26B-15-DT assigned to the 552nd BS/386th BG at Beaumont-sur-Oise in March 1945

UK remained at their bases – these were in turn assigned to the Ninth Air Force. As the 386th was one of the most experienced medium bomber groups in the ETO, it was selected to host the A-26 Project Squadron while it undertook combat evaluation missions with the aircraft in the autumn of 1944. After these had been completed, the Project Squadron relocated to Wethersfield and the 416th BG. The 386th BG continued to fly the B-26 Marauder from Great Dunmow, although A-26s were delivered to the 553rd BS to allow its conversion onto the new aircraft.

On 2 October 1944 the 386th moved to A60 Beaumont-sur-Oise, in France. From there the 553rd BS continued to fly combat operations alongside the group's B-26s. In January 1945, shortly after participating in the Ardennes campaign, the 386th's remaining three squadrons began conversion to the Invader, completing the swap on 21 February. The first all A-26 mission was flown that day. 48 hours earlier, Maj Myron Durkee had been credited with an Me 262 probably destroyed, thus demonstrating the nimbleness of the Invader in combat.

On 7 March the 386th attacked the marshalling yards at Wiesbaden with 30 A-26s. That same day Luftwaffe fighters were out in force, and shortly after completing their bomb run the 386th BG formation was attacked by 30 Bf 109s. They came at the bombers from astern in a line abreast formation known as a 'company front'. Attacks were made from positions ranging from 'five' to 'seven o'clock' and also from '12 o'clock'. They were pressed home with vigour and A-26 gunners claimed eight fighters destroyed. Three Invaders were downed, however, and two made crash-landings. 11 more A-26s were damaged by flak, fighters or both.

A-26B-15-DT 43-22373 saw considerable action with the 386th BG in the early months of 1945

The 386th BG moved from A60 to its new base, A92 St Trond, in Belgium, on 9 April. On the 21st it was one of three A-26 groups (the others being the 416th and the 391st), as well as the A-20-equipped 410th BG, to attack the marshalling yard at Attnang-Puchheim, in Austria. No flak or fighters were encountered, and the bombers

An A-26C from the 386th BG lands at St Trond at the completion of a mission in April 1945

Invaders from the 386th BG rest between missions at their dispersal at St Trond in the final weeks of the war in Europe

A 554th BS/386th BG Invader approaches its target over Germany on 20 April 1945. Note the flak bursts and the Invader formation ahead of this aircraft

A-26B-20-DT 43-22418 also served with the 386th BG

severely damaged both the yard and the railway line to southern Germany. Together with the 391st, 409th and 416th BGs, as well as the 1st Pathfinder Squadron, the 386th's final bombing mission came on 3 May when it participated in the attack on the Stod ammunition plant.

391st BG

The 391st BG was originally based at Matching (also known as Matching Green to members of the group), Essex. As one of the eight B-26 Marauder groups assigned to the Ninth Air Force, the 391st had flown its

This all-black A-26C was one of five Invaders assigned to the Eighth Air Force's 492nd BG in December 1944. Nicknamed 'The Carpet Baggers', the group was primarily equipped with B-24s (one can be seen in the background) which flew nocturnal missions from Watton, in Norfolk

The A-26s operated by the 492nd BG were personalised through the application of a playing card motif on either side of their nose. The Invaders were principally used to drop OSS agents behind German lines during night missions

first combat mission on 15 February 1944. In late September that year it moved to A73 Roye-Amy, in France, from where it continued operations. On 16 April 1945 the group moved to Y29 Asch, in Belgium.

The 391st had started the conversion to the A-26 late the previous month, and had completed it by the first week of April to become the last Ninth Bombardment Division group to switch to the Invader during World War 2. The 391st flew its first mission with the A-26 on 21 April when it participated in the attack on the marshalling yard at Attnang-Puchheim. On the 26th, in company with the 409th and 416th BGs, the 391st bombed Plattling airfield. Finally, on 3 May, the group attacked the Stod ammunition plant in Czechoslovakia, which was to be its last mission of World War 2.

The 397th BG also transitioned to the A-26, but it was still in the process of replacing its Marauders with Invaders when the war in Europe ended. Although the group saw no combat with the Douglas medium bomber, it flew the aircraft extensively from A72 Péronne immediately post-war. The group eventually returned to the US in December 1945.

The 10th Tactical Reconnaissance Squadron of the 69th Tactical Reconaissance Group almost certainly had several A-26s on strength in the final weeks of the war, these being flown alongside A-20s and B-25s from the group's bases at Nancy and Haguenau, both in France. The aircraft were used for post-mission bomb hit assessment photography of tactical targets that had been attacked by Ninth Bombardment Division aircraft.

Finally, the Eighth Air Force operated a total of five A-26Cs in support of the Office of Strategic Services (OSS), dropping their agents into Germany and occupied Europe. Two were initially used in place of Mosquitoes, which were not sufficiently large enough to carry more than one agent. Flown by crews (that included two navigators to accurately chart the course from the glazed nose) drawn from the Watton-based 25th BG(R), which was equipped with Mosquito PR XVIs, A-26C 43-22500 performed the type's first sortie – over northern

Holland – in this role on the night of 3 January 1945. Four nights later the aircraft was sent to northern Germany, only to crash-land with hydraulic failure at Watton upon its return. Two agents were dropped from 43-22524 near Berlin in the early hours of 2 March, after which all five Invaders were passed on to the Special Operations Group's 492nd BG at Harrington. 43-22524 failed to return from a mission on the night of 20 March, and this proved to be the Invader flight's only casualty. The group's last A-26C mission was flown on 9/10 May.

The 47th BG at Grosseto, in Italy, was the only group to be equipped with the A-26 in the MTO. The unit operated a mixed fleet of A-26Bs and Cs from the autumn of 1944 through to war's end. Night intruder missions were routinely flown by the group, hence a number of its A-26Cs were painted black overall

47th BG

The only unit to see combat with the A-26 in the Mediterranean Theatre of Operations (MTO) was the Twelfth Air Force's 47th BG. Like groups in the ETO, the 47th was primarily equipped with the A-20, having first seen action in North Africa with the aircraft from late 1942. Examples of the A-26 started to reach the 86th BS at Grosseto, in Italy, in the early autumn of 1944, and it took nearly six months for all four squadrons within the group to switch to the Invader. While this was taking place, the 47th flew mixed A-20/A-26 formations in its round-the-clock campaign against enemy targets in southern France and northern Italy.

From September 1944 to April 1945 the unit specialised in attacking German communications facilities and supply routes in mountainous northern Italy. The Invader was used both as a fair weather day bomber and a night intruder, with the 85th specialising in the latter mission. The aircraft was also used to test the viability of ground-directed bombing in the MTO, 47th BG crews working closely with units of the 22nd Tactical Air Command, which operated a SCR-584 radio station near Bologna. These proved particularly successful in the Po River Valley between

Featuring an 84th BS motif on its nose, this A-26B was photographed at Grosseto just after VE Day. The 47th BG was reassigned to Seymour-Johnson Army Air Force Base, North Carolina, in August 1945

Formerly assigned to the 553rd BS/
386th BG, this aircraft was passed
on to the 305th BG after VE Day.
The group participated in Project
'Casey Jones' in 1945, which saw
vast swathes of Europe and North
Africa photo-mapped by USAAF
aircraft such as this Invader

21 and 24 April 1945 when, despite bad weather and rugged terrain, the
47th maintained operations for 60 consecutive hours, destroying
the enemy's transportation facilities in the area and thus preventing them
from conducting an organised retreat. The unit earned a second
Presidential Unit Citation for its exploits during this period.

Lt Charles V Wilson was a bombardier/navigator with the 86th BS
during the final months of the war, and he recalled;

'We had no particular aircraft assigned to us, but all were painted flat
matt black. A few of our A-26s had solid noses housing six 0.50-cal
machine guns, but most of them were equipped with bombardier noses
for missions such as those that I took part in. Our armament consisted of
two 0.50-cal machine guns in both the ventral and dorsal turrets operated
by the gunner, who rode in the rear of the Invader. However, half the
time we didn't even carry a gunner.

'Most of our missions were despatched to strike targets of opportunity.
These were usually enemy airfields, bridges, marshalling yards and motor
transport. On clear nights convoys could be sighted rolling along the
highways. We had some real hot spots too. In the area around Venice, for
example, we could always expect searchlights and lots of flak.'

Whilst equipped with the A-26, the 47th BG flew missions against
such targets as tanks, convoys, bivouac areas, troop concentrations, supply

The 344th BG was another B-26
group to receive A-26s immediately
post-war, this aircraft serving with
the 495th BS as part of the US Army
Air Forces in Europe. The group
moved from A78 Florennes/Juzaine,
in Belgium, to R75 Schleissheim, in
Germany, in mid September 1945

dumps, roads, pontoon bridges,
railway lines and airfields. The
group was one of the first to return
to the US following VE Day,
arriving back in North Carolina in
August 1945. It was then issued
with new A-26s and told to prepare
for a transfer to the Pacific theatre,
but the Japanese surrender halted
the move.

By VE Day A-26 groups in
the ETO and MTO had flown
11,567 combat sorties and dropped
18,054 tons of ordnance. Some
67 Invaders had been lost and
the aircraft credited with seven
confirmed aerial victories.

PACIFIC INVADERS

Although the A-20-equipped 13th BS of the 3rd BG had seen combat with the A-26 in New Guinea as early as July 1944, it was the 319th BG that was selected to become the first Invader group in the Pacific theatre. There is an interesting reason for this. At the time the 319th was flying combat missions with the B-25 from bases in Italy. The manner in which the group converted to the A-26 was different to that employed by Ninth Air Force light and medium bomb groups in the ETO. There, the method used was to stand the entire unit down from operations while it converted to the Invader, with the group remaining at its home field during the conversion.

Once conversion was completed the unit resumed combat operations with the new aircraft. This method had an advantage in that the group was kept in-theatre during the conversion and no time was lost while it moved back and forth between the training area and its operating base. A major disadvantage, however, was the fact that the group was exposed to enemy attacks while the conversion was progressing. There was also a prevailing sense of urgency to complete the conversion as quickly as possible and resume combat operations. The continuous arrival of new personnel and the departure of those who had completed their tour of duty also had an effect on the conversion. It was therefore decided to withdraw the 319th BG as an entire unit from the MTO and return it to the US so that it could be re-equipped with A-26s.

In January 1945 the 319th was transferred from the MTO to Columbia Army Air Field, South Carolina, for training on the Invader. All personnel were granted leave on their return home prior to reporting to Columbia Field. After the group completed its conversion training, the air echelon arrived at Hunter Field, Georgia, to receive new A-26s. The group transferred to the Pacific theatre a short while later. After a long period of travel time, the 319th arrived at its new home, Machinato Field, Okinawa, on 2 July. Aircraft and crews followed 13 days later.

The Machinato Field was, and still is, sovereign Japanese territory, just as Hawaii and Alaska are sovereign US territory. This means that when you stand on a street corner on Okinawa you are standing in Japan. The invasion of Okinawa in February 1945 represented the first time that Japanese forces had been called upon to defend their homeland from Allied troops.

Machinato was a new airfield built on the southwest portion of the island. The runway and parking aprons, orientated north and south, were a quarter-of-a-mile from the shoreline at an elevation of 100 ft.

The 319th BG acquired factory-fresh A-26Bs and Cs prior to departing Hunter Field, Georgia, for Okinawa in mid 1945. This aircraft is seen in Georgia shortly after it joined the group

The group's camp area was midway between the sea, the runway and the parking aprons. The land sloped downwards from the airstrip to the sea.

When the 319th arrived at Machinato, its personnel learned that the field was still under construction, with the actual airfield portion, comprising the runway, taxiways and hard stands, unfinished. The aircraft were therefore temporarily based at Kadena, near the centre of the island. The group flew five missions from Kadena while Machinato was being completed. Crews soon learned there would be more hardships associated with operations from Kadena. The latter was 15 miles from Machinato, so it was impractical to transport groundcrews to and from the field every day. As a result, a temporary camp, complete with a field kitchen, was established at Kadena near the parked 319th aircraft. For the first few days the groundcrews slept in the open until two-man tents could be erected.

If this was not bad enough, the ammunition dump at Kadena had been destroyed in an explosion a few days before the group's arrival, and the nearest bomb dump was now eight miles away. There was no equipment for handling the bombs, so this meant that group personnel had to lift ordnance from storage racks onto waiting trucks for delivery to Kadena.

During the group's first week on Okinawa it rained almost every day. This produced a thick mud that some veterans likened to wet concrete. It penetrated clothing, shoes and anything else that would cause difficulty for those working in it. Walking was difficult and slow, and the mud stuck to the men's legs. Driving vehicles around the base proved to be just as difficult for they routinely became badly bogged. Moving ordnance and fuel from the storage areas to the flightline was a near-impossible task, and extra manpower was required to get everything through the mud. While several men could lift a 500-lb bomb, the mud seemed to make it twice as heavy. Once they were delivered to the aircraft, groundcrews used cables and hoists stored in the bombers to load the ordnance.

Conditions were not that much better for the group personnel – or anyone else on Okinawa for that matter – when it was dry, for the wind blew dust into and over everything and anything in its path, including food, clothes, eyes and aircraft. But bad as the dust was, the mud was worse. To add to the difficulties imposed by mud and dust, the extreme heat was described by the crews as almost unbearable.

On 16 July 1945 the 319th at last flew its first A-26 combat mission from Okinawa, escorted by P-47s. This was actually the group's 494th mission since it had first entered combat in the MTO. The target was the marshalling yards at Miyakonojo, on the Japanese island of Kyushu. When the group arrived over the marshalling yards, they were obscured by the weather and the alternative target of Miyazaki airfield was bombed instead. Because of the distance involved in travelling from Machinato to Kadena, briefings were held at night or very early in the morning so as to allow crews to arrive at their aircraft on time. While flying from Kadena the group utilised a two-ship formation take-off, with the element leader and his wingman departing in the formation in which they would fly. This also reduced the time required to form up before the group headed to the target.

For the second mission, on 17 July, the group attacked Chiang-Wan airfield in China. Arriving over the target area at altitudes ranging from 9600 ft to 10,600 ft, crews found the airfield obscured by a solid overcast at 6000 ft. As a result crews bombed on their estimated time of arrival over the target. Shortly after release a small opening in the cloud revealed that the bombs had fallen within the target area. There were two missions flown the next day, both against Lunghua airfield in Shanghai. Bombing results were rated as excellent. The second mission was to the same target, and bombing results were also excellent.

Amongst the Invader pilots to deploy with the 319th BG's 439th BS was Lt Gene Ryan, who recorded the details of his missions in a diary. Ryan participated in the Lunghua attack, writing afterwards;

The 319th BG's unit markings were a blue tail assembly with a white number. Only a handful of A-26s were so marked, however, because of the speed with which the group deployed to the Pacific

'All bombs (12 100-lb GPs) hit the target area, which was the revetments and dispersal area at the southwest side of the field. Forty-eight ships were sent out by the group and one ship in the second wave was hit by flak, the gunner being slightly injured. Another ship crashed when the nose gear wheel collapsed on landing – no one was injured. Generally the flak was light, although there was supposed to be about 50 heavy flak guns in the area.'

For the next two days no missions were flown due to bad weather. Conditions improved enough on 21 July for the 319th to make its first low-level attack on two enemy tankers. Results were rated as good.

Although the A-26s had departed for the mission from Kadena, they returned to Machinato, as it had finally been completed. The airfield's runway was narrower than Kadena's so only single aircraft take-offs could be performed, but there was one benefit for the crews. As Machinato was newer there was not nearly as much dust here as there had been at Kadena.

On 22 July the target was Ta-Chang airfield, Shanghai, where the group encountered heavy flak rated as accurate up to 10,000 ft, but inaccurate beyond that range. No group aircraft were reported as having been hit, although Capt Tenney had a close shave. The group flew in a series of diamond-shaped formations of four aircraft, with the No 4 machine flying behind and slightly lower than the lead bomber. Without realising it, Tenney flew too close to the lead aircraft, putting him in the direct path of its heavy and excessive downwash. Tenney's fuel consumption proved to be far greater than that of the other aircraft in the formation because of this.

By the time the group had made its second run on the target at near maximum speed, Tenney had used almost three-quarters of his fuel. He was not certain that he would have enough to make it back to Okinawa, and during his return flight Tenney dropped out of formation, reduced power and began a shallow descent. As he arrived over Kadena the gauges for both fuel tanks registered empty.

As usual the traffic pattern was crowded, so in an effort to conserve fuel he kept his gear up until he turned onto final approach. However, as

Machinato airfield was built from scratch in the southwestern corner of Okinawa island, and the 319th BG was the first unit to move in on 21 July 1945. A handful of A-26s, and a lone C-47, can be seen on its dusty ramp in this aerial view

he neared the runway he discovered that he could not lower the nose gear. Tenney kept pulling on the emergency gear lever, but the nose gear failed to lower. With little fuel, and the nose gear stuck in the up position, Tenney had no choice but to land and hold the nose up as long as possible while attempting to get as far along the runway as he could before lowering the nose and force-landing. The propellers and the nose were damaged by the time the aircraft had finally come to a halt, but the bomber was quickly repaired and returned to flying status. No one on board was injured, including a ground officer who had gone along 'for the ride' on the jump seat in the cockpit. When the fuel level in the tanks was checked it was discovered that only ten gallons remained.

Gene Ryan commented in his notes that 'This mission was about our maximum range at medium altitude for a formation. It was an 1180-mile round trip that lasted five-and-a-half hours'.

Another aircraft also returned from the mission with the nose gear up for lack of sufficient fuel to go around. The failure of A-26 nose gears on Okinawa was caused by coral dust and stones getting into the actuating mechanism. The group subsequently changed its landing pattern so as to give crews more time to check the position of the landing gear. Nose gear failure was also experienced in the ETO, as mentioned earlier. This problem was never fully remedied, being caused more through environment than a design flaw.

Ta-Chang airfield was targeted once again on 24 July, but when it was found to be blanketed in low-lying cloud the group bombed Ting-Hai airfield, on Chou Shan Island, instead. Two other missions to the same target that day were recalled due to bad weather. On the 24th the 319th also bombed the marshalling yards at Izuma, Japan. Four days later the group targeted the airfield at Kanoya, which was obscured by bad weather, so crews dropped bombed on ETA. Results were unobserved. The airfield was attacked again later that same day, and this time heavy flak was reported but no aircraft were hit. Bombing results were rated as good, with the entire target area being covered. Ryan also noted that while Kanoya had a high concentration of anti-aircraft guns, 'the flak was fairly heavy but not too accurate, even though the field was heavily defended. It seems as if they didn't have enough time to input the data into the guns and fire. We bombed from 8000 ft to 12,000 ft, with a ground speed of nearly 300 mph. This was a maximum effort mission, and the group sent 36 aircraft to Kanoya both in the morning and afternoon'.

During the afternoon mission the A-26s had enjoyed a P-47 escort for the first time in eight days. The fighters were assigned to the medium bombers following the interception of a B-24 raid on Tzuiki the previous day by 20 to 30 enemy aircraft. A ground officer had also tagged along in the lead A-26 when Kanoya was bombed, and this was common practice in the 319th.

On 29 July the target was shipping in Nagasaki harbour, with the group sending 36 of its A-26s. Nagasaki itself had been placed on the 'do not attack' list by the US government along with other possible targets for the 509th BG to strike with the world's first atomic weapons. The restriction did not include shipping present in the harbour, however. The lead A-26 of one of the squadrons developed instrument problems so that both it and the ten aircraft in its box bombed the alternate target – the Izumi marshalling yards – which were completely obscured by cloud. The aircraft bombed on ETA with unknown results.

Lt Ryan flew this mission in another pilot's aircraft, as his assigned bomber, *Lethal Lady*, had suffered a burned-out voltage regulator and there were no replacements then available on Okinawa. Flying *Yankee Dee* instead, Ryan noted after his return to Machinato;

'The target at Nagasaki was very important, but the group as a whole didn't do too sharp. Our flight was the only one that hit a ship out of the seven odd transports that were in the harbour. We got two direct hits on a 10,000-ton tanker that was burning when we left the target. The rest of our bombs hit the adjacent docks and warehouses. Many of the ships had to drop on ETA at the secondary target due to malfunctions and some personnel error. Thirty-six ships went out, each carrying six 500-lb GP bombs. The flak was rather light but pretty accurate. One ship in the squadron picked up a couple of holes. We also dropped the usual propaganda leaflets. The mission lasted 5 hrs 20 min.'

Two merchant ships were left burning from the bombing, and near misses were observed around a large vessel.

The target on 30 July was Omura airfield, which was bombed from altitudes up to 11,000 ft. The results on the northern dispersal area were rated as excellent, with one large and several small fires observed. The bombs from two flights were also observed to hit the southern dispersal area, completely covering it. The lead flight of the second squadron was unable to identify the aiming point and bombed Izumi airfield instead.

Two missions were flown the next day, with the target for the first being the railway bridge at Tomitaka. However, bad weather over the primary and secondary targets meant that the group attacked targets of opportunity. Crews flying the second mission headed for the southeastern dispersal area of Kanoya airfield, which was also completely obscured by the overcast. They bombed on ETA from altitudes ranging from 9100 ft

The unnamed crew of a 439th BS/319th BG A-26C return to the line shack to drop off their flight gear after completing yet another mission over Japan in July 1945

83

up to 11,300 ft, with unknown results. Flak was reported as being very weak. Ryan noted of his fifth mission;

'This was the group's 13th A-26 mission to date, and so far only four ships have been holed. It is quite a record, for units have been losing a few B-24s and B-25s over the same targets due to flak The reason for our lack of losses is that we are exposed to fire for a far shorter period of time due to our greater speed.

'I flew *Billie* today, as my ship is still out of action. The target was changed at the last minute from two railway bridges to Kanoya main airfield. The swap was made after Intelligence reported that 70 Jap fighters had been flown in there the night before. We were to knock them out – a paratrooper landing is also expected on Machinato, so the infantry has moved in with field guns. Kanoya would have been a pretty hot target had it not been completely overcast. This meant that no fighters came up and there was very meagre flak. We dropped on ETA, so it's questionable as to where the bombs hit. It is probably a good thing no fighters came up, for all we had for escort was four P-47Ns. They escorted us all the way to the target and back again, which wasn't too bad. The bad weather then prevented missions being flown for a period of four days.'

On 5 August the group flew a low-level bombing and strafing mission against industrial and built-up areas along the waterfront of the southern part of Tarumizu, on Kyushu. The results were unobserved. The next day the town of Miyaka Jono was attacked and many small fires were started, with explosions that were seen to destroy buildings. Flak was reported as light and inaccurate in the target area, with no aircraft being hit, although 12 A-26s sustained minor damage from debris that had been thrown up from explosions while flying at low-level.

The experience of these two missions resulted in a number of recommendations about how future low-level bombing and strafing attacks were made. After the aircraft had fired their five-inch high-velocity aerial rockets, they had to fly directly over the point of impact to complete their bomb runs. This resulted in the formations flying through debris and mud that had been thrown up by the exploding rockets, which damaged the attacking aircraft. The recommendation was to avoid combined bombing and rocket attacks on the same run.

By separating the two forms of attack it would be possible for the formation to break away from the run after rocket release, thereby avoiding the point of impact. A-26 pilot Maj Kale had reported that as he was starting to pull up from his run, rockets from the aircraft ahead of him exploded as they hit the target building, causing a wooden beam to be thrown up into the air. Reacting quickly, Kale was able to fly *underneath* the beam and avoid being struck by it. Another pilot, Lt Oscar Riddle of the 438th BS, was not so fortunate. Debris from rocket explosions struck his aircraft

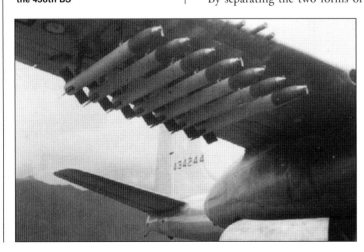

A close-up view of 5-in HVARs (High Velocity Aircraft Rockets) mounted beneath the outer wing of a 319th BG A-26B-50-DL. Typically, seven rockets would be carried under each wing, in addition to bombs that were always carried in the bomb-bay. This aircraft was assigned to the 438th BS

in both engines. One was completely disabled and the oil cooler on the other became clogged with debris. Riddle managed to keep control of his stricken aircraft, and for a considerable time flew just above stalling speed at an altitude of 200 ft. Several other A-26s dropped back to provide cover for him and to notify Air Sea Rescue should he have had to ditch his damaged aircraft.

Lt Ryan recalled, 'Yesterday they ran a low-level mission and about a dozen ships picked up holes and dents from the debris of their own rockets. Oscar Riddle came back about 450 miles on a single engine.

'Every morning at 0300 hrs the Japs have been sending down a few aeroplanes. They just seem to fly around and get shot at, and very seldom do any damage. We usually get out of the sack and watch the ack-ack. This afternoon a photo ship came over at about 40,000 ft, so I guess they'll be down again tonight. Some of the fellows have dug slit trenches.

'Flew my own ship today and it wasn't running too sharp. No radio and the right engine ran bad – after landing it stopped while I was taxiing down the runway. Among other things the nose wheel wouldn't come down the first time.'

On 7 August the group undertook its longest mission in the Pacific theatre when it flew 1140 miles to attack Tsuiki airfield in northern Kyushu. The bombing results were rated as excellent. The group had an escort, and although enemy fighters were seen, no encounters were reported. Gene Ryan flew on this mission, his sixth, and described it in his mission notes;

'Today was really a long mission. We hauled 12 260-lb frag bombs 1140 miles to dump them on Tsuiki airdrome. This field is on the northeastern tip of Kyushu, and we were over the island for an hour. We expected fighters but none came up. They must be in sad shape or holding back, for as usual our fighter escort didn't show up. Our bombs hit in the target area, but in the meantime they had moved the 70 ships that were supposed to be down there. I think the group is going up again tomorrow. The weather was clear over the target. It was pretty bad at the field when we took off. Weather is our biggest problem. The flak was very light and none of the 36 ships were hit. They briefed us for none at all. Three bursts hit pretty close right under our flight. The flight lasted six hours, which is too darn long for one pilot. I had 160 gallons of gas left when I landed, which is more than most of the ships had. One of these days the field will be closed when we get back and some one will have to ditch out here on the reef.'

8 August saw Tsuiki airfield bombed once again, and post-mission aerial photography showed that 100 per cent of the target area

Aircraft of the 319th BG pass over Machinato after forming up prior to heading to Japan on one of the group's early missions in July 1945

had been covered by ordnance. The next day's target was the eastern dispersal area of Kanoya airfield, with the group being escorted by P-51 Mustangs. Bombing was accomplished from altitudes ranging from 10,000 ft to 15,000 ft, with results being rated as excellent.

It was on this mission that crews reported an interesting occurrence. As the group flew towards the target, three unidentified aircraft were observed to the right of the formation, approximately three miles from them at 9000 ft. During the briefing for the mission, the 319th crews had been warned to stay clear of Fukuoka and Nagasaki, but they were not told why. The bomb run was flown in a northerly direction and the group executed a 180-degree turn to the left to return to Okinawa. The crews reported that just as they were making the turn they observed a brilliant flash of light and then saw a large dust cloud rising to 35,000 ft. To the crews it appeared as if a town about 20 or 30 miles away was burning, and the cloud was the smoke from the fire.

After the 319th landed at Okinawa, crews learned that what they had seen was the detonation of the atomic bomb dropped on Nagasaki 100 miles from their formation. It is possible that the aircraft seen by the group were the B-29s heading for Nagasaki to drop the second atomic bomb. Gene Ryan was on this mission, and his notes read as follows;

'Bombed Kanoya main airfield on Kyushu again. This time we had the right bombs for the job. We carried 20 120-lb frag clusters. The bombs hit in the revetments in what the colonel said was "the best area coverage of frags he had ever seen". The target was clear, although the surrounding area was completely overcast. The bombardiers in the four waves (36 ships) each took about a minute-and-a-half to complete their runs so as to make sure that we "cabbaged" the field this time. The flak was very light but fairly accurate. Two bursts hit pretty close behind and knocked the ship up about 30 ft. No holes, but two dents in the tail. The group always "breaks" after bombs away so they have very little chance to throw up any accurate flak.

'The target was changed at the last minute from a field further up the island, as the Twentieth Air Force didn't want us flying as close to Nagasaki as we were going to. It seems Nagasaki is scheduled for an "atomic" today. Last night I saw the photo-recon pictures of Hiroshima.'

Ryan does not, however, record his impression of those photographs, or of the atomic bombings.

On 10 August the 319th flew another low-level mission against military installations at Kumamoto, on Kyushu. Flying in four waves of eight aircraft, 32 bombers hit the target. The results were reported as effective, with numerous fires and explosions being observed. While no rocket attacks were made on this mission, 12 aircraft were damaged, mostly by debris from the explosions. The attack by the first wave of A-26s resulted in poor visibility caused by fires and smoke from the resulting explosions. Four of the Invaders were involved in minor mid-air collisions due to the smoke, but all 32 aircraft returned safely to Machinato airfield.

This 319th BG aircraft made a belly landing at Machinato after its gear malfunctioned upon returning from a mission. Note the rocket mounting pylons under the left wing

The pilot of A-26B-50-DL 44-34272 *PRINCESS PUD* carries out a forced landing at Machinato on 10 August 1945 following a mid-air collision with another 319th BG aircraft during a mission to Kyushu. Note bent right propeller, which the pilot had to feather after the collision

That night an innocent misunderstanding was to have tragic results for all personnel based on Okinawa. At approximately 2115 hrs Armed Forces Radio announced that Japan was suing for peace in general accordance with the dictates of the Potsdam Declaration. This news was interpreted as an announcement of Japan's surrender, and was toasted with alcohol from long-hoarded bottles. It was also greeted by shouts of joy and by the firing of almost every gun on the island, as well as those of many of the ships anchored offshore.

While the tracers from all the gunfire made for a spectacular sight, the joyful celebrations were tinged with tragedy. During the indiscriminate gunfire, five US personnel were killed by stray rounds, while a member of the 439th BS/319th BG was wounded in the arm by a spent bullet or a piece of shrapnel.

But 11 August brought with it confirmation that the war was not quite over. 36 of the group's A-26s were sent to bomb Tosu marshalling yards, and it was reported that their bombs struck a roundhouse, causing it to explode, as well as leaving numerous fires blazing in the target area. All aircraft returned safely to Okinawa, and no enemy fighters were encountered. The following morning the assigned target was the northwestern dispersal area of Chiran airfield. Although the weather was poor, hits resulting in fires in the target area were reported by the crews. Gene Ryan described the morning mission, and the events of previous nights, in his mission notes;

'Everyone thought the war was over the night before last, but obviously it isn't. The celebration was like nothing I have ever seen before. Searchlights, flares, Very pistols and every type of weapon from a 0.45-cal (the standard issue firearm for US service personnel) to a 5-in (naval and anti-aircraft) gun was going off. Someone said one of the boats even fired a couple of salvos of rockets. There were five people killed and 16 injured. Our operations officer got shot through the arm with a carbine.

'The group ran a mission yesterday, and we were the only bunch besides the B-25s that hit Japan. The "heavies" must have taken the day off. Today the group ran a maximum effort mission, sending out 32 ships in the morning and afternoon. I flew the morning mission and we bombed Chiran airfield, on Kyushu, with 20 120-lb clusters (80 frags). The target was covered with about seven-tenths cumulus and our squadron was the only one that hit the target area. The squadron bombardier only took a ten-second run. The flak was light and not very accurate. The mission

A-26B *LETHAL LADY*, flown by Lt Gene Ryan, returns from bombing Chiran airfield, on Kyushu, on 12 August 1945. This proved to be the last combat mission flown by the 319th BG in World War 2

was rather short, lasting 4 hrs 10 min. We didn't have any fighter escort as usual.

'Tomorrow, another maximum effort is planned, with every pilot flying – 48 ships in the morning and afternoon. The reason for these missions is to neutralise any enemy effort to mass ships on the southern airfields for a possible operation against us while the terms of surrender are being enacted. No one is happy about flying since the war is supposed to be over.'

On the afternoon of 12 August the group flew another mission against Kanoya airfield. The weather during the flight to the target was good, but when the crews arrived over the airfield an enormous build-up of cumulus cloud directly overhead completely obscured it. The group bombed the alternate target and returned to Okinawa. Lt Ryan's comment that the 'war is supposed to be over' was somewhat prophetic. The missions flown on 12 August were indeed the last flown during by the 319th BG in World War 2, although at the time none of the group's personnel knew it. The unit had completed 20 missions in total without suffering a single loss in combat.

3rd BG

Although the 3rd BG flew the A-26's initial combat evaluation missions in July 1944, it did not convert to the aircraft at that time. In fact, conversion to the Invader was never the intention, and the group continued to fly its A-20s in combat operations as part of the Fifth Air Force. Based at San Jose, on the Philippine island of Mindoro, the group started transitioning to the Invader in the early summer of 1945, and it did not complete its conversion until after the surrender of Japan. For the final weeks of the war the group flew both A-20s and A-26s in the offensive against Formosa, attacking airfields, ports, gun and troop emplacements and local industry. Operating at low-level, the 3rd BG's A-26s flew the USAAF's final mission over Formosa on 12 July when they attacked a sugar refinery.

The group moved to Okinawa on 6 August in preparation for the assault on Japan, and it flew a few missions (including a strike on an aircraft factory at Tarumizu) prior to the war ending. On 8 September the 3rd BG transferred from Okinawa to Atsugi air base in Japan, where it served as part of the occupation forces.

A formation of 3rd BG A-26Bs is pictured in flight over Japan during the winter of 1945. The 3rd BG did not convert to the A-26 until after the end of World War 2 in September 1945. The group's A-26s were built without the lower gun turret

341st BG

Activated in India on 15 September 1942, the 341st BG was equipped with B-25 Mitchells and sent into combat in early 1943 against Japanese ground targets in central Burma. In January 1944 the group was transferred to the Fourteenth Air Force, based in China. There it concentrated on anti-shipping strikes at sea and along China's inland waterways. It also attacked ground targets in Canton and in French Indochina. In the summer of 1945, the first of nearly 100 A-26s began arriving at Fenni, in India, for the 341st. From late June, crews were transferred from the group's Yangkai, China, base to Fenni to make the transition. Sufficient crews had made the switch by late July for the following entry to appear in the group history;

This 3rd BG A-26B made a belly landing at Okinawa in September 1945. This group was the first to fly olive drab-camouflaged Invaders

'From the distance came the muffled roar of approaching aircraft. The sound became louder in swift crescendo, and low! In the thin soup overhead there appeared three formations of a type of aircraft never before seen in the China Theatre. Nine A-26s, circling and peeling off to land, had arrived in China after their crews had completed a rigorous six-week training period at Fenni, India. More graceful and compact than the now discarded Mitchell, the Invaders barrelled down in rapid succession to nine perfect landings. This was an event worth seeing. The old order was changing before the eyes of the hardy ones who braved the cold chilling rain and persistent mosquitoes – the bomb group which had made history with the now almost obsolete B-25 was having its face lifted. It was a time for rejoicing and also for a little sadness, for the Mitchell was a "ding hao" ship and a true friend to all the men who knew her well. It was a time for gladness, because the A-26 symbolised a new phase in the war against the only remaining enemy, the phase that would spell defeat for the tailspinning Japanese.'

Frustratingly for the 341st BG, the enemy surrendered before it could give the A-26 its combat debut in the China-Burma-India theatre. In October 1945 the group flew its brand new aircraft from India to Germany and handed them over to the 344th BG at R75 Schleissheim.

The end of World War 2 brought the A-26 Invader's brief combat career to an end, or so it was thought, because it also brought the cancellation of large numbers of Invaders, including new models under development. A total of 2529 aircraft had been built, with the last example being handed over to the USAAF on 31 August 1945.

Although first flown in July 1942, the A-26 did not become operational until November 1944, limiting its opportunity to distinguish itself in combat, even though it was the fastest US bomber of the war. In the words of a 1950s Douglas advertisement, the A-26 'had the speed and manoeuvrability of a piston-engine fighter'. With its slim fuselage, graceful lines and huge nacelles housing a pair of 2000 hp R2800 radials, it certainly looked the part. Yet brief though it was, the A-26's World War 2 service was still enough to establish it as an effective combat aircraft, liked by its crews despite the niggling defects. The Invader was, however, to distinguish itself in another way – by participating in more conflicts than any other combat aircraft type. World War 2 was followed by service in Korea and Vietnam, but that is another story.

APPENDICES

NINTH AIR FORCE A-26 BOMB GROUP CODES

386th BG Codes	391st BG Codes	409th BG Codes	410th BG Codes	416th BG Codes
552nd BS – RG	572nd BS – P2	640th BS – W5	644th BS – 5D	668th BS – 5H
553rd BS – AN	573rd BS – T6	641st BS – 7G	645th BS – 7X	669th BS – 2A
554th BS – RU	574th BS – 4L	642nd BS – O6	646th BS – 8U	670th BS – F6
555th BS – YU	576th BS – O8	643rd BS – 5I	647th BS – 6Q	671st BS – 5C

CAMOUFLAGE AND MARKINGS

The initial prototypes of the A-26 were delivered in what was then the standard finish of olive drab upper surfaces over neutral grey undersides. Production aircraft were delivered in natural metal finish devoid of any paint apart from required (or desired) markings.

A-26s assigned to ETO units were supplied in the same natural metal finish as those delivered later to the 319th BG and other units in the Pacific. Each of the units assigned to the Eighth and Ninth Air Forces in England used an identification code in the form of either two letters or one letter and one number. The squadron code was applied to the fuselage forward of the national insignia on both sides. The individual aircraft letter was applied aft of the national insignia. For example, on the left-hand side, 'F6' (national insignia) 'H', and from the right-hand side, 'H' (national insignia) 'F6'. The width and style of the code letters, as well as the position of the aircraft letter, varied even within the same unit. Due to the limited space for the individual letter, it was quite often applied slightly higher than the other letters and national insignia on the fuselage.

Project Squadron and 416th BG

While attached to the 386th BG, the aircraft assigned to the Project Squadron displayed the yellow tail band and group code letters used by the unit. The main reason for this is believed to be the need to avoid the aircraft appearing to the enemy as a new type. After the evaluation missions had been completed, the Project Squadron began converting the 416th BG onto the A-26. At that time the Project Squadron's aircraft were also assigned to the 416th. While operating the camouflaged A-20, the 416th had applied a white stripe along the rear edge of the rudder of its aircraft. As the A-26 Invader was delivered in a natural metal finish, the group adopted a black stripe in place of the white one. With the A-26 being a new type in-theatre, invasion or D-Day stripes were applied to the lower fuselage aft of the bomb-bay. Not all the 416th's aircraft received these stripes, however, and photographs indicate two different styles of application. Some Invaders displayed the stripes starting from the rear edge of the bomb-bay, while others had them more or less centred on the lower turret.

409th BG

As with its A-20s, the 409th applied a yellow stripe to the rear portion of the rudder of its A-26s. Squadron and individual aircraft codes were applied in black on the fuselage on both sides of the national insignia in accordance with the practice adopted by units in the ETO.

410th BG

Although the 410th BG did not actually complete its conversion to the Invader during the war, the markings used on its A-20s were applied to the few A-26Bs that the group did deploy in combat for a short time. This marking was a coloured stripe applied to the rear portion of the rudder, similar to that used by the 416th and 409th BGs. The stripe was white, with four black squares, but the latter did not extend the full width of the white band, resulting in the appearance of a narrow white stripe along the leading edge of the rudder.

386th BG

When the 386th completed its conversion to the A-26 in the spring of 1945 it applied the same group tail marking to the new aircraft that had been displayed on its B-26 Marauders. This was a broad yellow band, edged in black, across the whole width of the tail, starting approximately 12 inches from the top of the tail. The same squadron codes used on the Marauders were also applied to the Invaders. Additionally, the 553rd BS painted its blue squadron colour on the engine cowlings of its aircraft, with some having the same colour applied to the entire nacelle.

391st BG

The A-26s of the 391st displayed the same triangle marking on the tail as had appeared on its B-26 Marauders. The yellow triangle featured a narrow black edge so that it stood out from the bare metal of the tail. The yellow paint used came from USAAF and RAF stocks, as well as, in at least one case, an unknown Allied ground unit. The group markings displayed a wide variety of shades of yellow as a result.

47th BG

Although most of the A-26s used by the MTO-based 47th BG were operated in natural metal finish, a handful were painted matt black overall to make them better suited to nocturnal interdiction operations. The group had no dedicated unit markings, instead applying two-numeral codes in black to the fins of their natural metal B-26s, and similar markings in white to the matt black aircraft.

3rd BG

No photographs of the A-26s used by the 3rd BG for the combat evaluation undertaken in June 1944 are known to exist. It is reported that they were flown in olive drab and neutral grey camouflage. It is not clear if the aircraft delivered to the 3rd BG in 1945, which arrived wearing the overall olive drab finish, were painted at the factory or once in the field with the unit. The 3rd BG applied markings to its Invaders that were similar to those displayed on its A-20s. Each squadron added its own colour to the tip of the tail, trimmed in white. A single large white letter was applied to the tail below the squadron colours, which were as follows – 8th BS yellow, 13th BS red, 89th BS green and 90th BS white.

319th BG

All aircraft delivered to the 319th BG arrived from the manufacturer in the standard natural metal finish, with their serial numbers (also called radio call numbers) painted in black on the tail. US Army Air Force regulations dictated that the entire serial number had to be painted on the fin, not on the rudder. At some time soon after receiving the aircraft, the group painted a large black three-digit number in the 500 series above the serial number. It is unclear exactly when this was done as photographs exist of the group's Invaders both with and without these three-digit numbers during the same timeframe. After its arrival in the Pacific the group began painting the tails of its aircraft in dark blue, as it had done with its B-25 Mitchells during its time in the MTO. A large white two-digit number was applied to the fin and rudder, with the serial number repainted in white. Only two of the group's Invaders are thought to have received the blue tails and white two-digit number. The first was A-26C '01', which was of course assigned to group CO Col J Holzapple. The other was A-26B '13'. During the course of research for this book, photographs were received by the author showing a third Invader ('08' 44-34555) in the process of receiving the group's blue colour at Machinato. The pictures show that the rudder was painted blue, while the remainder of the tail had yet to be resprayed.

COLOUR PLATES

1

A-26B-15-DT 43-22354 of the 669th BS/416th BG, A69 Laon, France, Spring 1945

This aircraft may have been one of the original 18 A-26s flown by the Project Squadron, as its individual letter 'S' differs from the standard application found on other Invaders in the 416th BG. The group's usual practice was to place the individual aircraft letter higher than the unit letters due to the narrowing of the fuselage near the tail. Named after Victor Appleton's main character in his pre-war series of juvenile adventure novels, the aircraft had participated in 48 missions by war's end. Remaining in the ETO post-war, it took part in the victory exposition staged beneath the Eiffel Tower by the United States Strategic Air Forces in Europe in August 1945.

2

A-26B-15-DT 43-22385 of the 668th BS/416th BG, A55 Melun, France, Spring 1945

Also assigned to the 416th BG, *BULA* displays the individual aircraft letter on the rear fuselage in the usual manner. Two pods, each containing two 0.50-in machine guns, can be seen mounted under the wings, although most photographs of the group's A-26s show aircraft with 'clean' wings, devoid of either gun pods or wing-mounted guns.

Like the previous Invader, this machine also saw plenty of combat with the 416th in the final months of the war in Europe.

3

A-26B-50-DL 44-34220 of the 437th BS/319th BG, Machinato, Okinawa, July 1945

This aircraft was one of at least two Invaders flown by the 319th BG to feature an all-blue tail. Although both machines were assigned to the 437th BS, blue-tailed B-26 'White 01' was assigned to the group CO. 'White 13', however, was flown by various 437th BS crews. All aircraft delivered to the 319th BG were in the standard natural metal finish, with their serial numbers (also called radio call numbers) painted in black on the tail. US Army instructions dictated that the entire serial number had to be painted on the fin, not the rudder. After arriving in the Pacific the group began painting the tails of its aircraft in dark blue, as it had done with its B-25s in the MTO. A large white two-digit number was applied to the fin and rudder, with the serial number repainted in white. Just three of the group's aircraft are thought to have received the blue tails and white two-digit number. The first was A-26C 44-35274 '01', assigned to group CO Col J Holzapple. The second aircraft was this A-26B 'White 13', and '08' 44-34555 also boasted an all blue tail.

4

A-26B-20-DT 43-22440 of the 84th BS/47th BG, Grosseto, Italy, early 1945

Aircraft '16' displays the natural metal finish that was usually seen on A-26s assigned to the 47th BG. This Invader was also adorned with the 84th BS emblem on its nose. Converted into a B-26C post-war, 43-22440 was one of 16 Invaders supplied to the *Fuerza Aerea del Ejercito de Cuba* in 1956 as part of the US Mutual Defense Assistance Program.

5

A-26B-60-DL 44-34486 of the 10th TRS/69th TRG, Y42 Nancy, France, Spring 1945

Aircraft '58' was assigned to the 69th TRG's 10th TRS during the final months of World War 2. Flying from the group's bases at Nancy and Haguenau, the A-26s were used for post-mission bomb hit assessment photography of tactical targets that had been attacked by Ninth Bombardment Division aircraft.

6

A-26B-15-DL 41-39198 of the Project Squadron (attached to the 386th BG), Great Dunmow, September 1944

Shown in the markings of the 553rd BS/386th BG, this aircraft was actually one of 18 Invaders assigned to the Project Squadron for the type's combat evaluation in the ETO. This aircraft remained with the 553rd BS after the Project Squadron had finished its evaluation in September 1944, the unit replacing the large 'R' on the bomber's tail with the 386th BG's broad yellow band (edged in black) across the whole width of the tail.

7

A-26B-15-DL 41-39198 of the 305th BG, A92 St Trond, Belgium, May 1945

Also seen in the previous profile, this aircraft had its solid nose replaced by a Plexiglas one and both turrets removed prior to being transferred as a 'hack' to the B-17G-equipped 305th BG at Chelveston, in Northamptonshire, in the spring of 1945. It had been declared war weary after more than seven months in action with the 386th BG. Although the aircraft retained its 553rd BS code letters, the group's yellow/black band was replaced by the 305th BG's similar marking in bright green, onto which was applied the group's famous black 'Triangle G'. The A-26 was used for familiarisation flights, the ferrying of air- and groundcrew between bases and for photo-mapping during Project 'Casey Jones'.

8

A-26B-15-DT 43-22343 of the 553rd BS/386th BG, A92 St Trond, Belgium, April 1945

This aircraft features an all blue nacelle which, along with its 'AN' codes, denotes its assignment to the 553rd BS. Several aircraft from this unit had engine cowlings painted in this colour. The 386th BG completed the conversion of its four squadrons

to the A-26 on 21 February 1945. One of a number of surplus Invaders fitted with a Plexiglas nose and re-designated a TB-26C second-line trainer within the post-war USAF, this aircraft crashed two miles from Tachikawa air base, Japan, on 9 October 1955 while attempting a go-around. Both crewmen were killed.

9

A-26B-20-DL 41-39264 of the 671st BS/416th BG, A55 Melun, France, December 1944

This aircraft displays the squadron and individual aircraft code letters in the thin style that was applied to several of the A-26 Invaders operated by the 671st BS from A55 in the winter of 1944.

10

A-26B-20-DL 41-39261 of the 643rd BS/409th BG, A48 Bretigny, France, December 1944

This A-26 came off the production line at Douglas Aircraft's Long Beach plant in October 1944. Issued new to the 409th BG in early December, the bomber was adorned with invasion stripes on the undersides of its lower rear fuselage as was common practice amongst Invaders operated by both the 409th and 416th BGs. 41-39261 was written off in a landing accident at A78 Florennes, in Belgium, on 14 March 1945 that also saw an RAF Mosquito and Halifax badly damaged.

11

A-26B-51-DL 44-34298 of the 89th BS/3rd BG, Atsugi, Japan, late 1945

'White E' was assigned to the 3rd BG when the group formed part of the Occupation of Japan Forces during the winter of 1945. The group's late production A-26Bs featured an eight-gun solid nose, both turrets and internally mounted wing guns. The aircraft were painted overall olive drab, with neutral grey undersides, prior to delivery to the unit.

12

A-26B-15-DT 43-22315 of the 670th BS/416th BG, A55 Melun, France, Autumn 1944

This aircraft, which was based at Melun and later Laon, displays invasion stripes on the undersides of its rear fuselage. These were applied to the A-26 for recognition purposes, as the type was then new to the ETO.

13

A-26B-55-DL 44-34374 of the 13th BS/3rd BG, Atsugi, Japan, late 1945

A-26B 'White N' was also assigned to the 3rd BG as part of the Occupation of Japan Forces in the winter of 1945. This late block aircraft was built without a lower turret and with an extra fuel tank installed inside the aft fuselage. It also features underwing mounts for rockets and drop tanks and wing-mounted machine guns. The 3rd BG applied markings to its Invaders that were similar to those displayed on its A-20s, each squadron adding its own colour to the tip of the tail, trimmed in white. A single large white letter was applied to the tail below the squadron colours, which were as follows – 8th BS yellow, 13th BS red, 89th BS green and 90th BS white. This aircraft was lost during a night interdiciton mission over Korea on 3 July 1951 whilst still serving with the 13th BS/3rd BG, its three-man crew being posted missing in action.

14
A-26B-50-DL 44-34272 of the 344th BS/319th BG, Machinato, Okinawa, July 1945
Christened PRINCESS PUD, this Invader was based at Machinato in July 1945. The 319th BG was the first and only group to fly the A-26 in combat in the Pacific theatre in World War 2, and it did not lose a single Invader to enemy action.

15
A-26B-15-DT 43-22359 of the 552nd BS/386th BG, A60 Beaumont-sur-Oise, France, April 1945
Nicknamed Stinky and adorned with a sharksmouth, this early flat top canopy A-26B was assigned to the 386th BG's 552nd BS and saw plenty of action from bases in France and Belgium in the final months of the war in Europe. When the 386th completed its conversion to the A-26 in the spring of 1945 it applied the same group tail marking to the new aircraft as had been displayed on its B-26 Marauders. This was a broad yellow band, edged in black, across the whole width of the tail, starting approximately 12 inches from the top of the tail. The same squadron codes used on the Marauders were also applied to the Invaders.

16
A-26B-40-DL 41-39590 of the 573rd BS/391st BG, Y29 Asch, Belgium, April 1945
The A-26s of the 391st displayed the same yellow triangle on the tail as had appeared on its B-26 Marauders. The yellow triangle featured a narrow black edge to enable it to stand out from the bare metal of the tail. 41-39590 was written off on 25 June 1945 when the aircraft crash-landed at B50 Vitry, in France.

17
A-26B-20-DT 43-22418 of the 554th BS/386th BG, A92 St Trond, Belgium, May 1945
Far from being flightless, Kiwi Boid completed a total of 30 missions by war's end. 'Boid' is the way a New Yorker from Brooklyn would pronounce the word 'bird', which may provide a clue as to the origins of the pilot of 43-22418 – or was he a New Zealander?!

18
A-26B-50-DL 44-34282 of the 319th BG, Machinato, Okinawa, July 1945
SWEET PETE was assigned to the 319th BG, although to which squadron remains unknown as the Invader lacked any distinguishing unit colours, markings or code letters/numbers. At some time soon after receiving the Invader, the group painted a large black three-digit number in the 500 series above the serial. It is unclear exactly when this was done as photographs exist of the group's aircraft both with and without the three-digit numbers during the same timeframe. 44-34282 was badly damaged in a forced landing at Machinato in early August 1945.

19
A-26B-51-DL 44-34323 of the 8th BS/3rd BG, Atsugi, Japan, Winter 1945
'White T' was based at Atsugi in the winter of 1945, and like most other aircraft delivered to the unit for service in Japan immediately post-war, it arrived in the olive drab over neutral grey paint scheme depicted here.

20
A-26B-20-DT 43-22415 of the 555th BS/386th BG, A92 St Trond, Belgium, May 1945
Christened Sky Chief and adorned with what appears to be a Devil's head on its nose, this bomber survived the war and was eventually one of 28 Invaders taken out of storage at Davis-Monthan AFB, Arizona, overhauled and then supplied to the Forca Aerea Brasileira in 1957-58. The veteran machine was scrapped in 1968 after being grounded following the appearance of wing spar cracks.

21
A-26B-56-DL 44-34343 of the 13th BS/3rd BG, Atsugi, Japan, Winter 1945
Aircraft 'Z' was another Atsugi-based A-26B that saw service as part of the Far East Air Forces' contribution to the army of occupation. Although experiencing only limited combat with the Invader in World War 2 during the aircraft's June 1944 combat evaluation, the 3rd BG was in the thick of the action with the aircraft in the Korean War from 27 June 1950 through to 27 July 1953.

22
A-26C-30-DT 44-35274 of the 319th BG, Machinato, Okinawa, July 1945
Aircraft 'White 01' was flown by the 319th's CO, Lt Col Joseph R Holzapple. Based at Machinato, Okinawa, this A-26C displays the third and final version of the identification markings used by the group. Lt Col Holzapple completed 99 combat missions totalling 423 hours with the 319th, which was dubbed 'Colonel Randy's Flying Circus'. His final eight sorties (33 hours) were made in this Invader against targets in both mainland Japan and China.

23
A-26C-20-DT 43-22555 of the 86th BS/47th BG, Grosseto, Italy, early 1945
Although most of the A-26s used by the MTO-based 47th BG were operated in natural metal finish, a handful were painted matt black overall (such as this aircraft) to make them better suited to nocturnal interdiction operations. The group had no dedicated unit markings, instead applying two-numeral codes in black to the fins of their natural metal A-26s, and

similar markings in white to the matt black aircraft. 47th BG squadrons also adorned their Invaders with individual unit emblems, as seen here.

24
A-26C-30-DT 44-35207 of the 646th BS/410th BG, A60 Beaumont-sur-Oise, France, June 1945
Although the 410th BG did not actually complete its conversion to the A-26 during the war, the markings used on its A-20s were applied to the few aircraft that the group did deploy in combat for a short time. This marking was a coloured stripe applied to the rear portion of the rudder, similar to that used by the 416th and the 409th BGs. The stripe was white with 3 black squares, but the latter did not extend the full width of the white band, resulting in the appearance of a narrow white stripe along the leading edge of the squares. This aircraft is unusual in having a three-digit number above its serial rather than a number/ letter code combination on the fuselage. 44-35207 was later equipped with a solid nose and sent to South Vietnam in January 1963 to serve with the USAF's 1st Air Commando Squadron as part of Program *Farm Gate*. 44-35207 subsequently crashed whilst on a test flight near Bien Hoa air base on 7 January 1964, both crewmen being killed.

25
A-26C-30-DT 44-35275 of the 439th BS/319th BG, Machinato, Okinawa, August 1945
'Black 578' was one of a handful of Perspex-nosed A-26Cs issued to the 319th BG to act as lead ships for the group. As with most Invaders issued to 'Colonel Randy's Flying Circus', 44-35275 bears no distinguishing group, squadron or personal markings.

26
A-26C-25-DT 43-22653 of the 572nd BS/391st BG, Y29 Asch, Belgium, April 1945
One of the last Invaders delivered to the 391st BG, this aircraft remained in post-war service with the USAF until the late 1950s, when it was retired. In 1963 the bomber was purchased by Idaho Air Tankers of Boise, Idaho, who converted it into a solid-nosed A-26B firebomber – a common modification for surplus Invaders sold to civilian operators in the early 1960s. Acquired by Reeder Flying Services of Twin Falls, Idaho, in 1966, the aircraft was bought by Canadian company Air Spray Ltd of Red Deer, Alberta, in 1981. One of a fleet of A-26s flown by this outfit, it was retired along with the rest of the Invaders in 2004 and placed in storage – it is still presently at Red Deer.

27
A-26C-15-DT 43-22486 of the 495th BS/344th BG, R75 Schleissheim, Germany, September 1945
This aircraft was assigned to the 495th BS/344th BG in the autumn of 1945 when the group moved to R75 Schleissheim as part of the occupation forces based in Germany. The 344th had retired the last of its war-weary B-26s just prior to being transferred to

Schleissheim from A78 Florennes. The group applied the familiar white/black triangle marking from its Marauder days to the tails of its A-26s.

28
A-26C-15-DT 43-22483 of the 552nd BS/386th BG, A60 Beaumont-sur-Oise, France, March 1945
This A-26C was used as a PFF lead ship by the 386th BG during the final months of the war in Europe.

29
A-26C-16-DT 43-22312 of the 553rd BS/386th BG, A60 Beaumont-sur-Oise, France, March 1945
Christened *Rat poison Jr.*, this aircraft displays the 553rd BS's assigned blue colour on its engine cowlings. 43-22312 was named after the unit's long serving B-26B Marauder 41-31606 *Rat Poison*, which was retained by the squadron as a hack after it had converted to the A-26.

30
A-26C-25-DT 43-22626 of the 856th BS/492nd BG, Harrington, Northamptonshire, April 1945
This aircraft was nicknamed *THE SAINT*, and it also bore a red 'U' on its tail inspired by the codename of a fictional spy from a popular novel at the time. 43-22626 was one of five A-26Cs flown by the Special Operations Group's 492nd BG from Harrington in the last two months of the war. These aircraft had been transferred to the group from the Watton-based 25th BG(R).

COLOUR SECTION

1
The subject of Profile 8, A-26B-15-DT 43-22343 flies in close formation for the benefit of the camera. This shot was taken during a sortie from St Trond in April 1945.

2
These 552nd BS/386th BG Invaders were also photographed at St Trond between missions, again in April 1945. The aircraft in the foreground is a late-build A-26C.

3
Featured in Profile 29, A-26C-16-DT 43-22312 was flown by Maj Stewart Marquis (seen here standing in the cockpit of the bomber). His navigator, Capt R H Denison, poses in full flight gear (including his parachute) in front of the aircraft. This shot was taken at St Trond in April 1945.

4
An A-26B of the 552nd BS/386th BG has its engines run up at St Trond prior to departing on its next mission from the Belgian base.

5
Aircraft from the 553rd BS taxi out at St Trond at the start of a squadron-strength operation in April 1945.